D0712776

CONVERSATIONS WITH THE FATHER

CONVERSATIONS WITH THE FATHER

A Memoir about Richard Matheson, My Dad and God

CHRIS MATHESON

PITCHSTONE PUBLISHING
DURHAM, NORTH CAROLINA

Pitchstone Publishing
Durham, North Carolina
www.pitchstonebooks.com

Printed in the USA
First edition

Library of Congress Cataloging-in-Publication Data

Names: Matheson, Chris, author.
Title: Conversations with the father : a memoir about Richard Matheson, my dad and God / Chris Matheson.
Description: Durham, North Carolina : Pitchstone Publishing, 2022. | Summary: "Screenwriter and author Chris Matheson shares memories of his dad, famed horror and science fiction writer Richard Matheson"—Provided by publisher.
Identifiers: LCCN 2022000901 (print) | LCCN 2022000902 (ebook) | ISBN 9781634312325 (hardcover) | ISBN 9781634312332 (ebook)
Subjects: LCSH: Matheson, Chris. | Matheson, Chris—Family. | Matheson, Richard, 1926-2013. | Fathers and sons—United States—Biography. | Authors, American—21st century—Biography.
Classification: LCC PS3613.A8262 Z46 2022 (print) | LCC PS3613.A8262 (ebook) | DDC 813/.6—dc23
LC record available at https://lccn.loc.gov/2022000901
LC ebook record available at https://lccn.loc.gov/2022000902

Cover image: the author and his father on the set of The Night Strangler *(1973)*

To my Mother,
in so many ways the coauthor of this particular story.

I

My father was the horror and science fiction writer Richard Matheson. He wrote many books and movies, among the best known being *I Am Legend* and *The Shrinking Man*. He wrote several classic *Twilight Zone* episodes, including "Nightmare at 20,000 Feet" (also known as "the one with William Shatner and the thing on the wing.") He wrote Steven Spielberg's first movie, *Duel*, the famous "Enemy Within" episode of *Star Trek*, and the time-travel love story *Somewhere in Time*. Dad was a very accomplished and gifted writer. He was also in many ways a wonderful father.

An early memory: I'm three years old and our family is at Disneyland. Dad and I are walking through some sets from the 1961 movie *Babes in Toyland*, which have been placed in the Opera House on Main Street. ("Great Moments with Mr. Lincoln" would later fill the space.) These sets are tremendously exciting to me; to enter into the world of this movie which I love so much, to enter into the main character Tom's life, to be near his beautiful girlfriend Mary—it's all thrilling. It's also terrifying, however, because one of the sets is the dark and foreboding "Forest of No Return." I want to go through the forest very much, but I'm quite frightened of it. So I simply stand at the edge of the forest for a long time, unable to go in, but definitely not wanting to leave either. I just stay there, immobilized. And Dad waits with me. He's at Disneyland, a place he likes a lot. (He and Mom first went there not long after it opened in 1955; they also, hilariously, went to Knott's Berry Farm on their honeymoon. Much later, Dad admired the "Haunted Mansion"; he always said that the giant ballroom filled with waltzing ghosts was the most interesting and beautiful thing in the park.) But while the rest of the family is having fun going on rides, Dad stands with his wavering and unsure three-year-old son at the edge of the "Forest of No Return" for at least an hour.

Another early memory: I'm four. Mom is sick in bed and I'm going out somewhere with Dad (to a movie possibly?). I feel happy and excited about that. I always felt happy and excited about being with Dad. If he was going to the market or the post office or the hardware store or wherever, I wanted to go with him. I loved him and wanted to be like him. I thought he was the best father ever. I was never close with my mother. Suffice to say, we didn't click. I didn't click with my three older siblings either. Dad was pretty much it for me. But Dad was enough. He was the one I wanted and needed.

On summer camping trips, when we'd leave our house in the middle of the night to get an early start, Mom and my siblings would climb into sleeping bags in the back of our Chevy camper and crash. I alone would sit upfront with

Dad, talking as we drove north through the middle of the night up Highway 101. We'd talk for hours, easily. Sometimes we'd talk about baseball, specifically the Dodgers, who we both loved. (Dad had loved them since he was a kid growing up in Brooklyn.) Dad always liked players he considered "canny"—not necessarily the most physically gifted ones, but the cleverest. In the late 1960s, that was Claude Osteen and Maury Wills; in the 1970s, it was Tommy John and Dusty Baker. Other times Dad would tell me scary ideas he had for stories. I remember one night speeding along an empty highway and Dad casually saying, "Wouldn't it be strange if we looked out the window and saw a man running alongside the camper right now, staring in at us?" It gave me the chills at the time; honestly, it's still creepy fifty years later.

Sometimes, in an offhand way, Dad would offer advice: the creative life needs to be lived cautiously, Dad would always say. (He seemed to assume I would do some kind of creative work.) Money needed to be spent carefully, never recklessly. Money for a creative person was freedom, Dad said. Therefore, to try to impress people with the car you drove or the clothes you wore or the restaurant you ate at was ridiculous; rather, focus on the freedom to create.

Dad and I were alike, he often said, and that was partially because we were both Pisces. Dad put a lot of stock in astrology, and the fact that we were born under the same sign was meaningful to him. It meant that we understood each other, that we were natural allies; it explained the natural affinity between us.

When the family played charades (which we did, quite often), I always found a way to be on Dad's team. I could often guess his answers off extremely minimal clues: "Movie! Five words! Third word, small word! And, if, but, of? Of! Three Days of the Condor?" "Right. Fifteen seconds." It went like this many times. Dad and I were in synch—we looked at the world the same way.

And of course I loved this. Being like Dad, having him *see* me as being like him, it felt wonderful and I cultivated it. If Dad liked a certain food, I learned to like it too. Dad loved liverwurst, braunschweiger, and chopped liver, so as a kid, I did too. Dad loved baseball; I became obsessed with the game too. Dad loved to act: I did too. (In 1976, we played father and son in Eugene O'Neill's *Ah, Wilderness!*) Mom and Dad were among the founding members of a theatre group in the community I grew up in; Dad became the group's first "comedy star." When I was nine, Dad played the villain, "Egbert Van Hoback," in the group's very first production, a musical melodrama called *Curse You, Jed Smith*. I'll never forget Dad's astounding first entrance. Dressed all in black, his beard dyed jet black, Dad swooped onto the stage, cape trailing behind him, and began to sing a song that he'd written.

I'm Van Hoback, they'd better go back!
Cuz when I come on the scene, then things go bad.
I'm Van Hoback, I SAID VAN HOBACK!
I am evil, I am mean, I am a cad!
There is nothing I would not stoop to, no depravity

or depth on which I frown!
I'm a dirty rotten plotter, an utter stinking ROTTER!!
I'M VAN HOBACK,
THE MEANEST MAN IN TOWNNNNN!!

I watched, amazed and thrilled. Dad was a star, people loved him, and they were right to, because he was funny. Fifteen years later I directed Dad in the same community theatre's production of *Our Town*. He played Editor Webb, Emily's father, and he was good, especially in his awkward pre-wedding conversation with soon-to-be son-in-law George Gibbs. Dad got tons of laughs in this scene.

Dad liked to make people laugh. He was a bit of a natural comedian in that sense. There are old 8 mm films of a "comedy routine" Dad would do every Christmas Eve, where he was trying to hang a bunch of stockings on the mantel but no matter how hard he tried, one of the stockings would invariably fall to the floor. As Dad got increasingly frustrated, more of the stockings would start to fall, until finally they would all fall and Dad, utterly discombobulated and wild-eyed, would topple to the floor too.

When I was about five or six, Dad came up with a bedtime game called "Tickle and Punch" that he would play with my sister Alison and me. "Tickle and Punch" was actually a series of little games played on my parents' bed while Mom sat and watched. Among the games were "Traps," in which Dad would clamp his hands around our wrists or ankles and not let us go, "the Tickle Brothers," in which the eponymous brothers (i.e., Dad's fingers) would tickle us while Dad speed-talked in a high-pitched voice ("We are the Tickle Brothers and we are going to *tiiiiiccccckkkllee* you!"), and "the Grumpy Old Man," wherein Dad would pretend to be an irritable old codger trying to take a nap and Alison and I would pester him until he woke up. "Hey wake up, old man." "Hunh? Leave me alone, you terrible children." "Wake up, old man, come on, wake up! WAKE UP!" "EERRGGGHHH!!" All these games were punctuated with childish laughter and also the occasional changing of pajama bottoms, because I sometimes laughed so hard that I literally wet my pants. I loved "Tickle and Punch" that much.

The part of "Tickle and Punch" that was the funniest though was "Captain Sock." The Captain (aka Dad's foot) was the captain of some kind of a ship. He was boastful, bombastic, and utterly dismissive of Alison and me: "I am the mighty CAPTAIN SOCK, ruler of the Seven Seas and you two are nothing but horrible CHILDREN!!" The game consisted of us trying to pull the sock off Dad's foot while Captain Sock shrieked with rage and disbelief. "I tell you I am the magnificent CAPTAIN SOCK and you will NEVER EVER SUCCEED!" he would bellow. Then as we started to pry the sock off, Captain Sock would start to completely freak out. "STOP WHAT YOU ARE DOING! STOP THIS MINUTE! I SAID STOOOPPPP!!" When we finally yanked Dad's sock off, as we invariably did, and held it up, empty and deflated, Captain Sock's voice would slowly shrink away like the Wicked Witch of the West after she's splashed with water:

"I, the great and awesome Captain Sock, am *defeeeeeeaaaated* by two horrid little children, ohhhhhhhhhhhhh!!"

When I was ten or eleven, Dad and I would take a little yellow pad and hand it back and forth, taking turns drawing and writing the most absurd little things we could possibly think of, basically creating nonsense together. I remember one drawing Dad made: it was of a woozy-looking military man, looking like he'd just been hit in the back of the head with a shovel, stars circling around his head. Behind the military man, an old man sat on a toilet. Dad's caption for the drawing: "Slap-happy cappy with crap-happy Pappy." I wish I'd kept the drawing; it was fantastic.

Dad and I would sometimes spend whole days together. We'd play eighteen holes of golf, stopping for lunch after nine. Dad was a good golfer, steady and consistent. I, on the other hand, was terrible, impatient and often furious with myself. We never kept score. Dad didn't want to. He said it would ruin the fun. Periodically, as we golfed, Dad would stop, close his eyes and take a long deep breath, exhaling slowly. He loved the outdoors, fresh air. After we finished golfing, we'd drive home, change clothes, and go out to "get a bite to eat," as Dad put it. (Loves Barbecue on Ventura Blvd. was a mutual favorite.) After that we'd go to the movies, often for a double feature.

A specific memory: It's 1977, I'm eighteen years old, Dad and I are out golfing. I'm driving our cart. We never walked; we always drove. I always drove, that is. Dad always let me, and I of course liked to drive fast, or as fast as you can in a golf cart anyway, 15 mph maybe? I take a turn too fast and Dad flies out the side of the golf cart and, because we're driving along the edge of a fairly steep hill, he starts toppling down it, yelling, "Oh! Oh! Oh!" as he does. I stop the cart, feeling terrible about what I've done but also—OH MY GOD—this is just about the funniest thing I've ever seen in my entire life. I instantly start laughing and I can't stop. I'm laughing so hard that I'm crying as I watch Dad tumble down the hill and finally crash to a stop. At the bottom, Dad slowly gets up and looks at me—he sees me laughing—and he starts to laugh too.

Dad loved to laugh. He laughed easily and often. Sometimes he laughed so hard that his face turned red because he couldn't breathe anymore. When Dad saw something he thought was funny he would erupt in gales of laughter. And I loved laughing with him. The things Dad thought were funny, well, I thought they were funny too. I remember Dad howling with laughter at Blake Edwards' *A Shot in the Dark*, when Herbert Lom's Commissioner Dreyfus cut off his own thumb because of his extreme agitation regarding Peter Sellers' Inspector Clouseau. "I just cut off my thumb," Lom says quietly, eye twitching. Dad loved Laurel and Hardy in *Another Fine Mess* and Harold Lloyd in *Safety Last*, and he adored the stateroom scene in *A Night at the Opera*. He seemed delighted by the gradually escalating ridiculousness of this scene—the way Groucho happily invites everyone into the stateroom no matter how crowded it gets. "Do you want a manicure?" "No, come on in!" "Is my Aunt Minnie in here?" "If she isn't, you can probably find someone just as good." "Say, is it my imagination or is it getting crowded in here?" Groucho finally asks, just before Margaret Dumont shows up and opens the door and everyone pours out.

Dad wrote scary things, but he didn't seem to much like them. Scary movies often upset him. We avoided seeing *The Exorcist* for close to a year for this very reason. (Dad did like Val Lewton's 1940s horror films and the 1957 French *Diabolique*. He was also a big fan of *Vertigo*. Dad liked telling the story of the time he almost got to work with Alfred Hitchcock on *The Birds*. In their meeting, Dad suggested—Val Lewton-style—not showing the birds very much. "We should keep them hidden and ominous for as long as possible," Dad had said. At that point Dad shifted into a funny impersonation of Hitchcock, sadly shaking his head and muttering, "Oh no, my dear boy, no no no." Then Dad would laugh and say, "I still think I was right!")

Dad wrote horror and science fiction but what he seemed to truly love was comedy. Through my teens, we avidly watched *All in the Family*, *Mary Tyler Moore*, *Bob Newhart*, *Sanford and Son*, and *The Carol Burnett Show*. Later, Dad took us to see *Blazing Saddles* and Richard Pryor's concert films. Dad doubled over with laughter at *Start the Revolution Without Me*, especially when Hugh Griffith's pathetic King Louis XVI wandered forlornly around a party in his idiotic-looking chicken suit, murmuring apologetically to anyone who would listen, "I thought it was a costume party." He had, overall, excellent taste in comedy.

One more memory: It's 1968, I'm nine years old. A large group of people, mainly adults, is playing games at our vacation cabin in Lake Arrowhead. The game we're playing is called "Dictionary." A dictionary is passed around and each player in turn finds a word that no one in the group recognizes. People then make up false definitions for the word, and after the fake definitions are all read aloud, the group votes on the most plausible-sounding fake definition. The word we were playing was "intaglio," and my made-up definition was "A man who blows out blind men's cigars." Upon hearing this, Dad burst out in laughter. When he then learned that it was me that had written the definition, he looked down at me with delighted surprise. I remember feeling overwhelmingly proud and excited at that moment. I had made Dad laugh, hard.

2

But there's another side to this story, another side to Dad.

When I was sixteen years old, Dad announced that he was planning on living to be 257 years old. Where exactly this notion and precise number had come from I had no idea at the time. (Now I do have a pretty good idea; it came from a book Dad had read and fallen for—more on that book to come). From my standpoint, Dad just suddenly started talking about how he was going to live to be 257 years old. He didn't really do anything to achieve this longevity. He didn't exercise more or eat better or anything really. What he did do was purchase a tent-like "pyramid" (in reality, a cheap metal framework covered with a thin plastic sheet) and occasionally lay inside it on the living room floor for 15–20 minutes, presumably deriving "pyramid power" from it.

Some obvious realities in my family when I was growing up: People could communicate psychically; we had all lived before, numerous times; ghosts, spirits, poltergeists, and haunted houses were absolutely real; you could communicate with the dead by holding a seance. Also: There was a thin silver cord that connected your body to your soul. You might stretch this cord if you astral projected, but the silver cord would not actually break until you died. At that point your soul would float up out of your body and gaze down at your dying self.

As a kid, I knew what "ectoplasm" was. I accepted that, yes, psychics actually did sometimes manifest this viscous substance from the their noses or mouths, and it sometimes did take on the appearance of a human being. I remember asking Dad about it.

"Is ectoplasm a real thing, Dad?" "Oh sure, ectoplasm is absolutely real." "Stuff that comes out of a psychic's nose during a seance, like snot or something?" "No, no, it's not like snot. It's more its own thing." "And it can actually take the shape of a dead person?" "Oh sure." "Which can then be spoken to?" "Yeah." "And sometimes it speaks back?" "Sometimes, yes." "And this is real, Dad?" "It's completely real, I've seen lots of evidence."

When I was a kid, if there was a pounding on a wall, that wasn't the house settling or the plumbing making a noise. No, that was a spirit, and probably an angry one too. If a parked car's window was mysteriously "missing," that wasn't because it had been rolled down at some point but because a poltergeist had taken it. If a light suddenly popped on in a closet, that was most likely the sign of a ghostly presence.

One of the magazines that was always lying around the house when I was a kid was *Fate: True Stories of the Strange and Unknown*. Here are some articles from the late sixties and early seventies when I was growing up: "Did Humans Tame

Dinosuars?" "Sex in the Spirit World," "Are Marriages Made in Heaven?" "How to Run Your Home Seance," "How to Resist Alien Abduction," "My Personal Banshee," "Message from the Sobbing Ghost," "How to Fight Demon Possession," "Battle of the Ghosts," "My Grandmother the Ghost," "ESP Revives Dead Plant," "Cats Go to Heaven," "How to Make a Magic Mirror," and "Astral Projection a Risky Process."

And the thing is—none of this stuff felt good to me. From the start, it felt weird, made-up, sickly in some way I couldn't have put into words at the time. I didn't exactly "disbelieve" yet. I didn't know enough for that. I didn't know much of anything, but I definitely knew that I disliked this stuff. I remember sometimes lying in my bed at night, turning on a little transistor radio and pressing it close to my ear, listening to the local news station and finding there was something extremely comforting about the fact that there was a real world out there, with real things happening in it. It wasn't all hidden and scary and bizarre.

I went to lots of bookstores with Dad when I was growing up. (He loved them, as I would assume all writers do.) I'd always drift to the sports section and happily look at baseball books. There was one bookstore I definitely did not like, though: the Bodhi Tree, the famous New Age bookstore off Melrose Avenue in West Hollywood. I didn't like the Bodhi Tree for three reasons: (1) It carried no baseball books; (2) The sound and smell and overall feel of it, the tinkly music and incense, all seemed icky and fake to me; and (3) Dad would occasionally be recognized by some alarming person who would stand too close to him and talk too loud and seem desperate and needy. There was one man in particular—his name was "Bongo"—whom I remember finding especially weird. Bongo wore vampire teeth that his dentist father had made for him, and he chomped them broadly while talking overexcitedly to Dad.

Dad wrote messages to himself on index cards: "Everything I do succeeds." "Every year I grow more successful." "I am increasingly calm, confident, and happy." He would write these commands to himself ten times on 3x5 index cards, then put the cards in his bedside drawer. Even though I more or less idolized Dad, there was something about those little index cards that made me uneasy. Why was Dad trying to talk himself into being confident? Was he not actually confident? The idea for the cards came from Dad's "success therapist," a man named Champion Teutsch. (I later went to see Dr. Teutsch on Dad's recommendation. I mainly just stared at his extremely buffed fingernails and his thick, chunky gold rings. I never went back.) Teutsch was a legitish scholar who made wildly overblown claims and thus came across as a charlatan. He claimed to have modified the genetic code, for instance.

In 1977 Dad wrote *What Dreams May Come*, a highly autobiographical novel about life after death. In the book, Dad's character, "Chris," dies in a car accident and, after a bit of time spent on Earth as a ghost, goes to heaven. Mom, unable to live without Dad, kills herself and, for that sin, is sent to hell. Dad travels to hell to save Mom and at the very last moment does so. As I read the book, I remember being thrown by it. Dad dies and goes to heaven, but Mom dies and goes to hell? "Why is that the story, Dad?" I remember asking him. "What else could it be?" "I don't know, maybe it could be flipped, like Mom could go to heaven and you could go to hell and then you'd have to escape hell to get to her, something like that?" "Oh no, that would make no sense at all." Dad sending himself to heaven and Mom to hell was definitely weird, I felt. (As was the fact that all us kids were left orphans in the book and Dad didn't even really acknowledge that—"they'll be fine," the book more or less shrugs.)

As I got older, Dad's New Age beliefs started to look increasingly implausible to me. Astrology would have been one of the first things I doubted because, well, the readings were all about me, and I didn't think what my Dad's astrologer "Franka" (who looked exactly the way you'd think she'd look) said about me described me very accurately. It mainly seemed like a bunch of overbroad generalizations that would basically be true of more or less anyone. Also, I started to wonder, why exactly would the location of the planets have any affect on my, or anyone else's, personality?

At first I didn't get into it with Dad. It simply wasn't worth it. If he found the fact that we were both Pisces meaningful, well, through my mid-twenties I saw no reason to disagree with him. Even though his beliefs didn't make much sense to me, I was close with Dad and that still felt good.

But the doubts were steadily growing.

About life after death, for instance. Why would there even be such a thing, I started to wonder. What possible purpose could it serve? Even more incomprehensible to me was the idea of ghosts. Why the hell would they exist? For what conceivable reason would the spirits of the dead continue to exist, floating around and scaring people? Supposedly, spirits were everywhere, but I never saw one. That's how it was, Dad explained; spirits never manifested to skeptics. Why? Because skepticism and disbelief interfered with their energy. Even daylight was harmful to the "finer matter" of spiritual emanations, it turned out. That's why they mainly appeared in dark rooms. Spirits, Dad explained to me, appeared only to those who already believed in them. "But if this stuff was actually real, wouldn't they appear to everyone, Dad?" "Not to skeptics, no." "But if it was true wouldn't skeptics be convinced?" "No, because they don't want to be convinced."

I thought this was laughable.

I won't lie; I had a motivation to laugh at these things. They had always upset me. I'd never liked them, never found them fun or exciting. Rather, I'd found them worrisome from the start. When I could laugh about them, it seemed to shrink them, put them in perspective. I was always a very anxious kid, always nervous about one thing or another. At some point (and I wish I could remember the exact moment but I can't) I discovered that when I laughed at things, I felt less scared of them. That of course made me want to laugh at things as much as possible. I wanted to watch funny things, read funny things, and, as I got older, try to make funny things.

In 1986, when I was twenty-seven years old, I got in a car accident. It wasn't a major accident, not at all, but my head did hit the windshield, causing me to see "stars." I was quickly released from the emergency hospital because I felt fine, but in the aftermath of the accident, I started to feel . . . strange—more emotional, more easily upset, and far more anxious. I began to have panic attacks for the first time in my life. I sometimes hyperventilated until I thought I was going to pass out. I felt I was a failure and a loser and I kind of hated myself. I felt a powerful need to get away from people, to be alone, to lick my wounds, I suppose. Among those I pulled away from at this time was Dad.

I would have thought beforehand—or certainly hoped anyway—that Dad would understand what I was doing. After all, he'd left his family behind in 1951 at the age of twenty-five and pretty much never looked back. I thought he'd get it. But I think my pulling away must have hurt his feelings, and I can see now how it could have. I'd always looked up to Dad and wanted to be as close to him as I possibly could. Now I wanted distance from him.

But as Dad got upset with me for needing space, well, predictably, that only made me need more space, which seemed to bother Dad even more. A quick downward cycle resulted, which did a tremendous amount of damage to our relationship in a very short amount of time.

The car accident did something else too. It made me, for the first time, start to get interested in religion. I'd had no interest up to the age of twenty-seven. I'd quite literally never set foot in a church of any kind. Now, feeling confused and worried, having apparently "shaken something loose" in my head, I started to look for "meaning."

I started to go into churches, and I instantly found them intriguing, different from anyplace else I'd ever been. I was affected by the deep meanings embedded in pretty much everything I looked at. "This is fascinating," I remember thinking to myself. "I definitely need to learn more about this." A few months later, I read the Bible for the first time. This reading did not, I found, enhance my estimation of Dad's New Age beliefs. I didn't find myself thinking Christianity was "true," not at all, but I did think it was beautiful in a way and had obviously inspired a lot of magnificent art. Dad's New Age stuff looked puny and overblown to me by comparison.

Dad wanted me to believe what he believed, to go along with his story. I had always been his boy, his greatest admirer, his true believer. Now I started to turn on him, disagree with him, even make fun of his beliefs. "Why do you not believe?" Dad started to demand of me. "What's wrong with you that you don't believe?" is what I was pretty sure he meant. "What's wrong with you that you do believe?" I started more or less responding. Our conversations, historically so effortless and enjoyable, started to grow tense. I didn't like Dad's worldview. I thought his ideas were stunted and fear-based. He thought I was angry and destructive. We both thought we were right, pretty much knew we were right. Dad sometimes blamed my astrological chart. I'm an "Aries rising," which to Dad explained my irascible, contentious nature. If Dad wanted to let me off the hook in years to come, in fact, or end an argument, he would attribute my skepticism to my chart. "It must be very difficult to be an Aries rising."

Growing up, all through my teens and into my twenties, I'd always felt that Dad believed in me. "Things come easily for you, Chris," he had often said. That wasn't true—things didn't come easily for me, not at all, but I liked hearing it, it always gave me a bit of confidence. Dad believed in me and that counted for a lot. By the time I was thirty, though, Dad's refrain had changed. It was no longer, "Things come easily for you, Chris," but rather, "I hope you know what you're doing, Chris." Which, honestly, I didn't. I made tons of mistakes of many different kinds, but hearing Dad's grim "I hope you know what you're doing," well, it never helped.

I didn't look at Dad the same way anymore and that caused him to not look at me the same way anymore. He became more critical of me as I became more critical of him. At a certain point I felt like Dad's ability to be a father to me just sort of ran out. He couldn't be, or maybe didn't want to be, a father to a doubting, skeptical young man who didn't buy his ideas and didn't seem to want to either. Had Dad ever actually believed in me, I began to wonder? Or had he only believed in me because I believed in him?

3

By the 1990s I'd completely turned against Dad's ideas and I didn't keep it to myself. I thought his New Age beliefs were ridiculous, and I expressed that opinion regularly. Listening to me, Dad would exhale sharply and stare at me with his cool green eyes. (I always thought Max von Sydow would have played Dad very well, the cool and forbidding northernness of him.) I was never going to believe what Dad believed anymore and he knew that. On the other hand, I was never going to convince him he was wrong either. We were stuck, increasingly annoyed by what we both seemed to regard as the other's stubborn unreasonableness.

As we kept arguing, all the good feelings we'd built up over so many years started to burn off. We didn't go to the movies together or watch Dodgers games or play Scrabble anymore. All we did was disagree about, well, the meaning of life, really. When I was younger I'd always imagined that Dad and I would have a close relationship all the way through, that we'd be one of those happy father-son pairs who enjoyed each other's company at every stage of life. I would have liked that very much. I'm sure Dad would have too. But it didn't go that way for us. By the mid-nineties, the old feelings were gone. We didn't dislike each other exactly, but we definitely irritated each other. We were cold to each other now. Dad was full Norwegian and I'm half Norwegian, so there was a lot of chilliness on both sides.

And now we get to *that* book.

At some point (as I said, presumably at the Bodhi Tree, somewhere in the 1970s) Dad picked up Harold Percival's magnum opus *Thinking and Destiny*. "*T&D*" became a hugely important book for Dad—in effect, his "Bible." He talked about the book often, believing that it got at the "truth" of things. When we argued, he would often refer to it.

"Have you read *Thinking and Destiny* yet, Chris?"

"Not yet, Dad. It's really long."

"You need to read it, then we can talk more meaningfully."

"So I have to read *Thinking and Destiny* before we can talk about this stuff, Dad?"

"You can't truly understand my belief system until you read *Thinking and Destiny*."

In my mid-thirties, I finally read the book. I'd known Dad believed in some pretty weird things growing up, obviously, but reading *Thinking and Destiny* . . . it was weird beyond anything I was prepared for. In the foreword, Harold Percival shares his key interests and insights. At the age of seven, he writes, he knew that he wanted to live forever. While other children played (which young Harold apparently had no interest in, he generally seems to disapprove of play), Percival thought about eternity and immortality. At the age of twenty-four, Percival tells us that he had an epiphany. Crossing 14th Street in Manhattan, he suddenly, in his words, "apprehended reality." In an instant, that is, Percival knew . . . well, kind of everything. Time didn't exist and neither did space. At the center of everything was "Consciousness, the Ultimate Reality." One of Percival's favorite moves is capitalizing words. He presumably did so to convey importance: "The Light of an Intelligence is a Conscious Light . . . related to the Triune Self." It's completely unnecessary and wildly pretentious—not much different *from italicizing too many words* or using too many exclamation points!!!

Percival knows the things he says are true. They were revealed to him so therefore, without any evidence at all (and Percival never has any of that), he can simply tell us over and over what Absolute Reality is. Chapter II of the book (not "2"—*T&D* is high pomposity from start to finish) is modestly titled "The Purpose and Plan of the Universe." Underneath its facade of "loftiness," however, *Thinking and Destiny* is small and unimaginative. You're born blind because you caused someone else to go blind in another lifetime; born deaf because you listened to lies in a previous lifetime. If you "accidentally" lose a limb because a surgeon mistakenly amputates your arm, well, guess what? That was no "accident": you wanted that arm amputated to make up for your misdeeds in a previous lifetime.

I thought *Thinking and Destiny* was nonsense—total bullshit. And as you might imagine, our conversations about the book did not go well:

I read *Thinking and Destiny*, Dad.

Oh, that's good.

Actually maybe not, because I have to say I can't understand how you believe this book is, like, the truth.

Because it is the truth, Chris.

Well, Percival says it's the truth, but that doesn't mean it actually is.

I think you didn't understand it. Thinking and Destiny *is the greatest book I've ever read, by far.*

Percival offers no evidence for anything he says, Dad. Like none at all, ever.

Of course he does.

No, he asserts things, essentially says, "This is how things are." And some of the stuff he writes is just flat-out nuts, like saying that before recorded history people had flying boats and rode fish around underwater and then a bit later there were flying people, some of whom were green, and somehow I'm pretty sure all this led up to Atlantis.

It did, yes.

NONE of this shows up in any archaeological record, Dad.

The archaeological record could easily have been destroyed by volcanoes, Chris.

Well, if that's true, then basically anything is possible.

Sure, that's right.

The point is, given everything we know, there's zero reason to believe any of this stuff is true, Dad.

Look, I don't know if every single specific thing Percival writes is true, okay?

That's good.

But that's not what matters, what matters is that the larger picture is true.

The larger picture being that everything in the universe is basically a projection of human thought?

Yes.

Everything is a product of our thinking? You believe that, Dad?

Oh, absolutely.

The universe began over 14 billion years ago, Dad, how exactly did human thought create that?

There are levels of existence you don't necessarily understand, Chris.

So you're saying human thought did create the universe?

Basically, yes.

But human beings didn't even exist for the first 99.999 percent of the universe's life—they weren't even around until maybe a few hundred thousand years ago.

They weren't around on Earth maybe but their souls were around from the start.

And where were all these souls? In heaven?

I would think so, yes.

So from heaven all these souls caused the Big Bang?

Yeah.

And then these souls basically waited 14 billion years to finally show up as human beings?

First of all, the wait wasn't as long as you say. Don't forget, there was Atlantis.

I don't believe Atlantis existed, Dad.

You're wrong, it absolutely did exist.

Okay fine, for the sake of argument, let's say it did. That would add maybe ten thousand years to human history, at most.

It could be a hundred thousand years.

But we're talking 14 BILLION years, Dad.

The problem is—you read the book from a skeptical point

of view.

I read it, Dad.

You have to read something sympathetically, Chris, not scoffing at it the whole time. You didn't read it with an open mind.

Oh Dad, come on. Percival's a total fake.

How is he a fake?

He wants to act like his needs and fears play no role in what he's writing. He wants to remain totally opaque and hidden, like pay no attention to the man behind the curtain, when it's pretty obvious that the man behind the curtain is terrified of death and freaked out by sex. I also don't like Percival's idea that whatever bad thing happens to you, you basically deserve it.

Why not?

What could someone possibly do in a previous life that would lead them to die of a painful disease at five years of age, Dad?

I don't know. Something bad, I guess.

Something REALLY bad.

Yeah.

You don't think that's ugly?

I think a child dying for no reason at all is ugly.

I agree, it is, but them dying for some "reason," like they deserve it, is even worse.

You think it's better if these things are just random accidents, Chris?

I do, yes.

You think horrible things happening to children for no reason at all is less bad than there being reasons for it?

Yes, because the "reasons" always seem to end up blaming the victim. Some kid's experiencing horrible misfortune and he deserves it?

Or maybe he needs it. Your view of things makes everything meaningless, Chris. I see a larger purpose in things and you think my view of things is ugly?

I think saying a little kid deserves the excruciating disease that's slowly killing him is ugly, Dad, yes.

They chose it, that's different from they "deserve" it.

Right, they want their horrible disease.

They may need to learn something.

By dying horribly.

It's the way souls improve, Chris.

Through suffering.

Yes, exactly.

Well, it seems to me there's been a whole LOT of suffering in the history of the world, Dad. You'd think there would have been a bit more improvement.

It's actually YOUR beliefs that are ugly, Chris.

Why?

You can't even say that "morality" exists in any objective sense, can you?

I mean . . . no, I guess not.

So how can you say anything is morally wrong then? How can you even say the Holocaust was "wrong" in any absolute sense?

I mean . . . I can't, not in any "objective" way.

Well, that seems utterly horrendous to me.

I'm not defending the Holocaust, Dad. I'm just saying I think it's even worse if all those people were murdered for some "purpose," because what purpose could possibly justify it?

Then it's meaningless.

Bad things happen and I don't think we ultimately know why, Dad. I think life is mysterious in a way.

It doesn't have to be.

Maybe it does.

Maybe to you it does.

Maybe to everyone it does, Dad. Maybe that's just how it is. Maybe that's even part of the beauty of it in a way.

Life's not less beautiful if you understand it, Chris. It's actually far more beautiful. Percival's talking about huge things, Chris. I hate to say it, but maybe you're just not ready to understand them yet, that's all.

Jesus . . .

Maybe at some other time in your life you will be.

Or maybe I never will be, Dad.

For your sake, I hope that's not true.

It's all made-up, Dad.

Or maybe you just can't grasp it yet.

Or maybe you just want to grasp it.

Sometimes I think you're just disagreeable, Chris. But then I remind myself you're an Aries rising.

Sure, that's probably it.

It makes you very difficult to deal with because you always think you're right. But don't worry, you'll get there eventually.

I may not want to get there, Dad.

You'll still get there.

What if I never agree with you, Dad?

That would disturb me terribly.

It might happen, is the thing.

I truly hope not.

We stare at each other in intractable silence for a minute. Then I mutter something like, "Whatever, Dad," and we separate—until the next time we go at it.

4

Death is not the end, Chris.

I've never seen one decent piece of evidence that it isn't, Dad.

There's a mountain of evidence. You just don't seem to want to accept it. We definitely survive. There's no question about it.

Well, I think there is a question. But even if there wasn't, I don't necessarily see why survival after death would be a good thing.

Are you saying you don't want to continue to exist?

I'm saying that I accept at some point I won't because that's just the way things are.

It's not the way things are though.

I hope to get ninety years here. That seems like a pretty decent shot, long enough to have a family, do some work, see a few things, and then, you know, go. I don't look forward to death, it IS kind of scary to me . . .

It doesn't need to be.

But then I think to myself, literally everyone who's ever lived has died, ALL of them. I think we get our time here and after that it's time to move along and let others have a shot at it. What's so wrong with that way of looking at things, Dad?

It's not how it is, that's all.

What's wrong with it though, is what I'm asking?

It's too short. There's no chance to really learn or change.

But there is, Dad. Ninety years is a long time.

Wouldn't you like to have a chance to understand what Absolute Reality is, Chris?

I'm not sure I would, no.

You wouldn't?

I don't mind not knowing, Dad. I kind of like not knowing in some ways.

We don't have to be confused, Chris.

Maybe we do though, Dad, at least to a certain extent. And maybe that's not such a bad thing. Would you actually want to learn what "Absolute Reality" was?

Yes, of course.

Like how everything began, how it's going to end?

Sure, both of those things, and lots more. The true nature of things, Chris: Absolute Reality.

And you seriously believe you're going to know that?

We all are eventually, if we want to.

And what exactly would one do with that knowledge once one had it?

Work with it, obviously.

Doing what though?

What do you mean?

I mean, what would be the *point* of attaining knowledge? Here, on Earth, in this life, we have to survive and therefore knowledge has value. But if you were immortal, what good would knowledge be?

You're not looking at things correctly, Chris. If we just lived this one life and then died and that was it, life would be completely pointless.

Why would life be completely pointless, Dad?

Because we're more than that, Chris. Our lives mean more than that.

I actually think this life means a LOT, Dad.

Of course it does. All lives mean a lot.

I think this life means more to me than it does to you.

Why would you say that?

Because I think the ninety years or whatever I get here, that's *it*—that's my one and only chance to exist. I won't get another. It's literally 100 percent of my existence.

You're wrong about that.

Whereas for you that same ninety years is not even 1 percent. It's not even any percent. It's infinitesimal—this part of your existence is literally infinitesimal, Dad. Why do you think that's good?

What I think is that you don't understand my belief system, Chris.

My life feels important partially because it's all I have, Dad. The meaning of it seems somehow tied up with the limits of it, with the fact that it's going to end. I remember this quote I once read, "The essence of every picture is the frame . . ."

G. K. Chesterton.

Right, exactly, G. K. Chesterton. And the thing is, if you lived forever, there'd be no frame. I want to make the most of this life, Dad, not spend it worrying about some imaginary future.

It's not imaginary, Chris, that's what you're missing.

Well, no one's ever been there.

Many people have been there.

They say they've been there—they may think they've been there—but it doesn't mean they actually have been there.

No, they have been there. It's completely real.

I think it's all made-up, Dad. It seems totally obvious to me that it's all made-up, in fact. I also think it's an incredibly bleak view of existence.

Bleak?? How is it bleak?

Human life as a kind of exile during which we're trapped in these awful, disgusting physical bodies? That's bleak, Dad. I actually think life is wonderful. Trashing this life in order to build up these completely made-up, whatever, "heavens," I don't get that at all. Not to mention Percival's crazy ideas about what these heavens are like.

What's crazy about them?

The idea that we're all alone in our personal heavens?

Yeah, that's definitely true.

And you're OKAY with that?

Sure.

Doesn't that sound incredibly lonely, Dad?

I don't think of it that way.

If I was alone in heaven, it'd be more like hell for me. Actually worse, because at least I wouldn't be all alone in hell, right?

No, other people are definitely in hell with you.

I think I'll choose hell then.

Don't say that, Chris.

I'm just saying, Dad, given the options, I'll definitely pick hell.

Oh, Chris. Why are you so skeptical about everything?

I think it's good to be skeptical, Dad. There's an awful lot of bullshit in the world.

That's true, there is, but you have to be able to recognize what's not bullshit.

Like *Thinking and Destiny . . .*

Not only Thinking and Destiny. *Edgar Cayce too. Did you read him?*

Yep.

Did you like it?

Nope, I thought it was ridiculous.

Oh, that's terrible.

Sorry.

Tell me something, Chris.

Okay.

What exactly do you get out of all this disbelief? How does it in any way benefit you?

Well . . .

You always seem so tense and anxious, you always seem so upset.

It's true, I often am, Dad.

Maybe if you believed in something you'd feel better, did you ever think of that?

Maybe if I actually believed in it, sure.

You just have to want to believe in it, Chris, but for some reason, and I truly don't understand what it is, you don't seem to want to.

Well, first off, I'm not gonna pretend to believe things just because I think it's a good, whatever, investment. But it's more than that, Dad.

How so?

I actually think you're the one who's losing out.

What do you think I'm losing out on?

The ability to doubt, ask questions, be skeptical.

Oh, I'm very skeptical.

You can't possibly believe in this stuff and call yourself a skeptic, Dad. You're giving up your ability to think critically.

By saying we can be better, Chris? By saying we can move beyond what we are now and become something better? By believing that in time, we can actually attain knowledge . . . justice . . . beauty? By believing that eventually we can, in a sense, become love?

I don't know what to say, Dad.

You can improve, Chris. You can be who you want to be. You want to be less scared, less anxious? You can be. You want to be more successful? You can be that too.

Just by telling myself I am?

You could start out by writing some affirmations. Didn't Teutsch give you some?

He did.

"Everything I do succeeds" is a good, simple one.

But everything I do doesn't succeed, Dad. Not even close.

That's why I'm suggesting it, Chris.

You're saying I'd always succeed if I wrote, "Everything I do succeeds," what, twenty times a day? . . .

That would probably be enough, sure.

I just . . . I don't believe it, Dad, I'm sorry.

Oh, Chris . . .

Everything I do isn't going to succeed and honestly, I'm not sure I'd even want it to.

Why on Earth not?

I feel like I learn things from my failures.

You'd still learn things, Chris, but you'd be succeeding while you did.

I feel like I'm trying to . . . I don't know . . . figure something out here, Dad. It's a super-slow process and I'm definitely struggling with it.

I can see that.

I'm sure everyone can, but I keep trying and hoping that maybe someday, I don't know when, maybe never honestly, but maybe someday I will figure something out. I'll, whatever, "succeed," and that'll feel great.

Wouldn't you rather have more successes?

I want to earn them is what I'm saying, Dad, not just tell myself I'm having them.

Like you think I do.

Well, I mean . . . yeah. Also, given your belief system, I don't understand why "success" even matters.

It matters in this life.

Sure, but I mean in the bigger sense, thinking about "success" seems insignificant, given that you're eternal and all.

Why do you do this, Chris?

What do you mean?

I mean, what are you actually hoping to accomplish by attacking my beliefs like this?

What am I hoping to . . . ?

Are you hoping I'll stop believing?

Uh . . .

So that you can feel like you're right?

. . . I don't think it's just that.

Do you think you're doing it for me? Do you think I'd be better off if I didn't believe in all this, Chris? Is that what you think?

I guess so, yeah.

You think you're doing me some kind of service then by mocking my beliefs, like you're going to "free" me from my laughable New Age thinking by attacking it. Is that basically right?

I think if that ever did happen, you'd live more in reality, Dad.

Do you think it's somehow morally or intellectually "superior" to believe this life is all we have, Chris?

I do sort of think that, yeah.

You're obviously aware that the vast majority of people in the history of the world, the vast majority of people alive right now, believe in some kind of afterlife. You think they're all wrong? They're all wrong and you're right?

I think the way I look at things is probably closer to the truth, yeah.

But you don't actually know it's closer to the truth, do you?

Do I know it?

You can't know it, can you?

. . . Alright. No.

We're all dealing with fear here, Chris. We just have different ways of doing it, that's all.

I don't claim my way is "the truth," though, Dad.

You mock all the ideas you don't agree with, I'd say that makes it pretty obvious that you think you're right about things.

It's totally different.

You do have a "truth," Chris. You might not be aware of it, but you do.

But it's not like yours, Dad.

It's not like mine, that's true, but you have one. You're not some neutral, objective observer of life. You seem to like to make fun of things. That apparently makes them less scary for you; Fine. But that doesn't work for everyone. It doesn't work for me.

Right.

The truth is, I don't like the idea of dying, I don't like the idea of not existing. I want to exist and I've found a belief system that makes me very confident—EXTREMELY confident, in fact—that I will continue to exist. You want me to throw this whole belief system away just because YOU don't like it?

No, Dad.

What do you want then?

. . . I don't know.

To put me down?

. . . I don't know . . .

What did I do to you that I deserve all this scorn, Chris?

. . . Nothing, Dad.

Do you think other people's fears are funny?

I think the way people cover up their fears sometimes is funny.

You don't cover up your fears?

No, I definitely do.

And is that funny?

I mean, yeah, it probably is.

And would you like it if I made fun of you?

You're my Dad.

And you're my son.

Right, and kids make fun of their parents, you know, Dad?

I can't say I understand that . . . but you know . . . since I never had a father . . .

Right . . . I know . . .

Maybe what you're describing is part of having a father. You can laugh at him.

You know, I think that's probably right, Dad.

Okay then . . . sure . . . I just hate to see you so lost, Chris.

Try not to worry about me too much, Pop. I think I'm gonna be okay. Really.

Okay . . . that's good . . . I'm glad you feel that way.

Just like your way of thinking works for you, the way I look at things . . . it works for me, you know?

When you laugh, you're less scared.

Right.

And you like that. That's why you like to laugh at things.

Definitely.

Okay . . . Okay . . . Sure . . .

5

Again and again throughout *Thinking and Destiny*, Harold Percival informs us that one of the main things we have to look forward to as we spiritually progress is "a perfect sexless body." He uses the phrase literally dozens of times in the book. I remember reading this and thinking, "Why would anyone want to be sexless? Why would that be anyone's idea of perfect?" Percival never married, never had children. From reading his work, I'd wager that he died a virgin. Sexuality seemed to horrify him that much. Dad, on the other hand, was married for over sixty years and was the father of four children. I couldn't understand it.

Why would you want to be sexless, Dad?

That's a long ways off, Chris.

Right, but it's gonna happen eventually, right?

Eventually, yeah.

And it'll be a good thing when it does, right?

I think you may be too young to get it.

I'm thirty-five, Dad. I'm not that young. Also, you're not that old. You're in your mid-sixties.

At the stage of progression Percival is talking about there's simply no need for sex, that's all.

The whole goal of life, Percival says, is to move beyond sex, to the point that one's sexual organs literally disappear. Along with one's anus, for some reason.

Because you wouldn't eat at that point, obviously.

But I like to eat. Why would it be good not to eat?

Because it's closer to physical perfection, Chris.

I don't think it is.

Well, then, it won't happen to you.

Honestly, the whole book seems to revolve around how sex has turned us bad, Dad, degraded us. Percival doesn't even like flowers because he says they're too sexual! He says sex literally led to the existence of vermin. He says even having sexual thoughts can cause cancer.

Those who wish to can continue to have sex, Chris. It delays spiritual progress, that's all.

But if one wants to wander in the desert, one can, is that it?

It seems to me that you're the one who has issues with sex, Chris.

I do have issues with sex, Dad, you're right. The truth is, I've felt a ton of anxiety in my life about sex. "Am I man enough to satisfy a woman?"—all of that. Honestly, I've often doubted that I was. I've often been quite sure I wasn't, in fact.

I'm sorry to hear that.

Right, me too. But here's the thing, Dad: Sex can also be amazing.

Oh sure, sure.

If you're having it with the right person, which obviously is essential, sex can be like the deepest and most interesting game you could ever play. Why would anyone want to cut that out of their life? People who have sex literally have the mark of the beast on them, Percival says!

Only in the sense that sex leads to birth, Chris.

Which is bad.

Only because it leads to death.

Apparently the situation isn't utterly hopeless though. When sexual thoughts come, if you immediately think of the "Realm of Permanence," which I assume is heaven . . .

Yeah.

. . . Then you can at least begin the process of becoming a perfect sexless being. Percival doesn't even believe in love, Dad.

Oh no, he definitely does.

Marriage is unnatural, he says, improper and wrong. Love for oneself, according to Percival, that's the only true love.

Yeah, that's true.

Jesus, Dad, that's awful!

Why is it awful?

True love is only for oneself? You don't see why that's awful?

No, not at all.

It means we're all alone! It makes love meaningless, even for your kids! Percival obviously doesn't even like children. He talks about their "glazed eyes and their blank little faces." Kids aren't "empty vessels," or whatever the hell Percival calls them, Dad.

Children are alive, Chris. All Percival is saying is that their souls don't enter them until they're older.

That's just bullshit. I know my own kids, Dad, and they weren't EVER "empty vessels"! They had personality from the very start. Then Percival has the—I don't even know what to call it, it's not "balls," because he definitely does not have those—but let's say the nerve to give child-rearing advice. The main thing you have to teach your children, he says, is that they are not their body.

Right.

You should address them as "Conscious One." "Conscious One, you need to understand that you are not your body."

Yeah.

It's the stupidest thing I've ever heard, Dad. Who would actually say such a ridiculous thing to a little kid? You certainly didn't.

I hadn't read Percival at the time.

What, if you had you would have said that?

Maybe, I'm not sure.

I don't believe you would have said such a ludicrous thing, Dad.

Once again, I think you're missing the bigger picture here, Chris.

Which is what, Dad?

That our souls are eternal, that we're here to learn, and that we can learn if we'll only listen—and maybe stop making fun of things we don't understand.

Harold Percival is insane, Dad! He says in time not only

will we have perfect, sexless bodies, but we'll also have four brains, one in our pelvis, one in our abdomen, one in our thorax and one in our head! He says we won't have blood anymore, just "life currents," whatever those are! He says we won't breathe through our lungs anymore! Dad, you do see how crazy all this is, right?

Do you want to spend your whole life making fun of things, Chris?

I don't know, maybe, what if I do?

There's more to life than that.

Well, do you want to spend your whole life hiding, Dad, because there's more to life than that too.

Oh, I'm not hiding. This definitely isn't hiding.

I think it is.

This is reality, Chris. And I think you're completely wrong about Percival.

He's stunted, Dad. He's a pompous, overblown little nothing, trying to pass himself off as some kind of a "prophet."

Oh no no.

Dad, seriously. Why do you believe this guy??

But the truth is: Dad had his reasons.

6

It's extremely likely that both of Dad's parents, Bertolf Matthiessen and Fanny Svenningsen, were raised as Lutherans. Most Norwegians in the 1800s were. Until the middle of the nineteenth century, in fact, Lutheranism was the only legal religion in Norway and membership in the church was mandatory for everyone living there.

There's a lot of sin in Martin Luther's writing. His very first "thesis" states that the life of the believer should revolve around "repentance," and it's pretty clear for what: Our bodies, Luther writes, are "stench and filth encased in flesh." Our digestive organs are especially repulsive to him. According to Luther, God made mankind perfect, but because we—that is, Adam and Eve—pretty much instantly turned bad, our lives are wholly infected with sin. What we deserve is hell—we're that bad. Body hatred in Christianity goes back a long way obviously. Paul writes in Romans of mankind's "vile desires, and the consequent degradation of their bodies." Augustine writes in *The City of God* that we "pollute" each other with our perverted lusts. What Dad's parents grew up believing was rooted in dark self-hatred, specifically regarding the body and its sexual desires. Dad grew up, that is, in a family that had been steeped in guilt, repression, and shame for centuries.

At some point, presumably not long after she arrived in the United States circa 1908, Dad's mother, my grandmother, converted from Lutheranism to Christian Science, which was at the time the fastest growing religion in the United States, attracting hundreds of thousands of followers in the decades after its founding in 1879 by Mary Baker Eddy. Eddy's *Science and Health*, the central text of Christian Science, conveys the same sense of absolute certainty as Percival's *Thinking and Destiny*. "Christian Science presents the calm and clear verdict of Truth against error," Eddy writes early in the book. "It is the voice of Truth." (This last sentence falls under the heading, "This volume, indispensable," which I find hilarious. My favorite Eddy self-description: "Others could not take her place, even if willing so to do. She therefore remains unseen at her post, seeking no self-aggrandizement but praying, watching, and working for the redemption of mankind." The third person self-importance of this is pretty hard to top.) The question "Do you have any proof to back your claims up?" didn't ever seem to enter Dad's mind, in part because he'd been indoctrinated into this kind of belief as a child.

What Dad got out of Christian Science, the aspect of it that clearly resonated with him, was the idea that one has total control of one's own life. That which one doesn't like in oneself, one can simply change. Why? Because it's literally all in your mind. Sick bodies come from sick minds, and the only true cause of pain is thinking there's pain. Eddy tells the story of a faithful little Christian Scientist girl with a badly wounded finger who showed no pain at all. According to Eddy, the girl announced to her mother, "There is no sensation in matter," before bounding off with "laughing eyes." On the flip side, Eddy tells the story of a man who "bleeds to death" without actually bleeding at all, simply because he thinks he's bleeding to death. Thus, for Eddy, what doctors should tell patients is simple. If someone thinks they're sick, disabuse them of the notion. "You do not have cancer," the doctor should say. "It's only an illusion, a shadow which will soon flee before the light of truth." Mental illness should be handled the same way. "You are not in fact suicidal and it's incorrect for you to think that."

Dad's father Bertolf was a bricklayer. When Dad was eight, his mother kicked his father out for drinking, and Dad didn't see his father much from that point onward. When Bertolf did come around, Dad, turned against his alcoholic father by his mother, treated him coldly. Dad was haunted by a memory from his early teens: His father had come by on Christmas Eve and tried to give him five dollars (equivalent to something like a hundred dollars today), but Dad turned his father's money down. I remember Dad describing the stricken look on his father's face. Bertolf Matthiessen died not long afterward. Dad's final book, *Generations*, published when he was eighty-five, placed Bertolf's death at the center of the story. *Generations* was the last thing Dad ever wrote, the bookend to a spectacularly prolific career, and it ends with a plaintive question: "Why didn't my father want me?

Why didn't my father love me?" It's reminiscent in a way of John Lennon's devastating "Mother": *"Father, you left me, but I never left you. I needed you, you didn't need me."*

Dad was clearly fascinated by sex; it's everywhere in his work, one of his main subjects. Sex also clearly scared him, however. I'm not the first person to suggest that fear of women is the true subject of Dad's greatest and deepest book, *The Shrinking Man*. Consider the book's gauntlet of "female" threats: the cat, the little girl, the black widow spider, and (above all?) the wife's sexual needs. As the main character, Scott Carey, shrinks, he quickly ceases to be able to please his wife sexually. He can't be "a man" anymore and she pities him for it. "I'm not a boy!" he cries out to her at one point. "I'm not a boy!" But it's not just fear of women that pervades the book. An older man, thinking that Carey is a child because of his small stature, wants to molest him. (Dad was molested by an older man when he was fifteen years old, in 1941, the same year his father died.) Some older boys humiliate Carey, attempting to yank his pants down so they can see his shrunken penis. Men aren't safe either, the book says. No one is safe.

Fascination with and fear of sexuality permeate Dad's other books too. In *I Am Legend*, Robert Neville, effectively the last man on Earth, is nightly tormented by vampire women who slink around outside his house. The women strike "vile postures" to lure Neville outside. They are "lewd puppets," "lustful and bloodthirsty," flaunting their naked bodies at him.

In *A Stir of Echoes*, when Tom Wallace attains psychic powers, one of the most disturbing things he starts to encounter is his neighbor Elsie's sexual hunger. Elsie is slightly heavy, and Tom doesn't want to be attracted to her, but he is. "Come to me," Elsie's mind starts whispering to Tom. She "makes his flesh crawl." She is a "strength-draining incarnation of lust." Her ravenous mind nearly overwhelms Tom. (Two of Dad's short stories that similarly feature women mind-controlling men for sexual purposes are "Lover, When You're Near Me" and "The Likeness of Julie.")

Then there's *Hell House*, Dad's starkest exploration of sexuality. The primary power of Hell House lies in how it affects women: It makes them want sex. Edith Barrett has previously been repressed, even scared of sex. In Hell House, however, she begins to feel her own desires. "Make it hard," Edith whispers hoarsely to her (impotent) husband, Lionel. "For Christ's sake, make it hard!" Lionel gags, slams his head back and cries out, his face contorted in pain. The scariest thing in the book for Barrett would seem to be his own wife's sex drive.

Next Edith comes on to Fischer, a psychic. Fischer tries to snap her out of it. "It's the house," he tells her. "It's making you—." "*The house is doing nothing*," Edith sharply replies. "*I'm* doing it. Are you impotent too?" Fischer tries again to reach Edith. This isn't the "real" her, he insists, she's sleepwalking, dreaming. "Wake up!" he yells. "Don't tell *me* to wake up," Edith snaps. "*You* wake up!—you sexless bastard."

Meanwhile, Florence, the female psychic in the book, is repeatedly sexually attacked by the villainous Belasco's spirit and thus infected with Hell House's sexuality. "He's inside me,"

Florence moans after Belasco's spirit has raped her. "Fight it," Fischer urges her. (He's the only one who seems to know how to survive Hell House: Stay guarded, don't open yourself up, and for God's sake, avoid sex!)

"I want to fuck," Florence starts saying. "I want to fuck!" She's out of her mind, the book tells us. She attacks Edith, who is turned on by it. Then Belasco's spirit has anal sex with Florence. After that there's a threesome with Edith. "Vacuous abandonment," the book calls all this. "Wanton sexuality."

Hell House is obsessed with sex (it really could be called "Sex House"), but it's also extremely moralizing. There's a wild ambivalence on the page here. Dad can't stop writing about sex, but he also knows it's bad, very BAD.

I don't think Dad knew which way to turn sexually, who he was. I suspect that he might have been bisexual. It's obvious from Dad's work that he had a sexual interest in men. It's there in his first novel, *Hunger and Thirst*, written when he was twenty-three years old, and it's still there in *Generations*, written sixty-two years later. In a different time, with a different background, Dad might have enjoyed himself sexually in this world. Instead, he shut his sexuality down, then looked for a belief system that would tell him that shutting sexuality down was exactly the right thing to do.

Wanting to understand Dad better, I read his "popularization" of *Thinking and Destiny*, a work of "inspirational fiction" published in 1999 titled *The Path*. The plot of *The Path* is simple: A mysterious man shows up one morning in the main character's (basically Dad's) life and starts talking to him on his walks. The two men share a series of conversations. The "drama" of the book lies in its peculiar psychology. The main character, "Dad," instantly becomes obsessed with the mystery man. Not long after meeting him, he literally can't think of anything else but the man. "I knew you'd come," the man says to Dad as they meet one morning. "Was I that tranparent to him?" Dad thinks. Again and again throughout the book Dad "surrenders," "accepts," "submits," or is "obedient" to the man. Like a lonely and insecure teenage boy, Dad accepts everything the man tells him, never once (until the very end) asking the man what would seem to be a rather obvious question: Is there any evidence for these things you're telling me? (The answer would be no, by the way.) When the man touches him, Dad cannot even describe the feeling it gives him. He wobbles slightly when the man pulls his hand away. He's "hooked" and he knows it, "thrilled" by the man's mere presence.

Dad's excellent sense of humor deserts him in *The Path*. While the two men seem to share endless smiles and chuckles, nothing even remotely funny is ever spoken between them. The mystery man, in fact, is rather anti-laughter. And midway through the book he's explicit about why: Because skepticism and ridicule "interfere" with psychic phenomena.

When Dad thinks late in the book that he's offended the man and caused him to leave, he's horrified. "Please," Dad murmurs to himself, "please." He can't stand the idea of losing this man; it causes him "anguish" and "despair." At this point we learn, somewhat out of the blue, that Dad's character is actually married. "Wait, he's married?" I remember thinking to myself. "He's never mentioned his wife once." Does he tell her about these deep conversations he's having with a mysterious man he's having such powerful feelings for? Presumably not. We learn at the same time that Dad also has four children, a fact which in a way feels even more surprising. This man does not in any way feel like a father; he feels like a child. Dad loves the mystery man more and more. He thinks he's perfect now. Before long, the man is literally patting Dad on the head like he's a little boy.

On the second to last page of *The Path*, Dad finally asks the question I'd been waiting for him to ask the whole book: "How do I know what you've been telling me is true?" The man places his hand on Dad's shoulder, gazes into his eyes, and gives the big reveal of the book: "You're me," he says to Dad. The man, it turns out, is Dad's future, highly evolved self. The circularity is complete: The only person Dad will ever feel truly close to is himself.

The Path is a very sad book, I can now see. Dad had no father and he desperately needed one, desperately hungered for a father's guidance and approval, desperately longed for someone to reassure him and give him advice. And Harold Percival turned out to be a horribly perfect fit for what Dad needed. As I say, sad. At the time, however, in the late 1990s, the book horrified me. "This is who you are??" I remember thinking.

Around the year 2000 I wrote a short piece that I originally called "Mondays with the Lord," in which a character named

Gordon Whitehead strikes up a conversation with God. Even though the piece was overtly making fun of Dad's belief system, I decided to show it to him anyway. After all, Dad was incredibly smart about writing. Whenever he read my work, he offered insightful notes, often perceiving problems (and potential solutions) that I didn't see. I wanted his feedback because it was so valuable. But there was obviously something else at work too: I was poking at Dad with this piece. I assumed he'd be irritated and we'd have an argument. Maybe that's even sort of what I wanted to happen.

But it's not what happened.

Dad liked the story, enough so, in fact, that he not only offered up some helpful ideas but also even wrote a few jokes for me to include in it. I never did anything with "Mondays with the Lord." It sat on a shelf for twenty years. Then, in 2020, going through some old stuff in the basement, I found both the piece and Dad's notes on it. Reading through them, something struck me: I had been making fun of Dad and he had gone along with the joke, encouraged it, even contributed to it. I was surprised at the time, but then again, maybe I shouldn't have been.

Because that other side of Dad, the side that loved comedy, believed in comedy—well, it came out at some pretty damned surprising times. Consider the conclusion of *Hell House*: The solution to ending Belasco's long haunting of Hell House turns out to be, of all things, *making fun of him*. Belasco was a fraud, Fischer realizes. He pretended to be physically large but was actually small, so small, in fact, that he surgically had his legs removed and had fake ones attached. The true problem at the center of Hell House turns out to be profound insecurity and GIGANTIC overcompensation. And the true answer to this problem turns out to be . . . LAUGHTER!

These are Dad's notes on the book:

> He suggested the title "Chattin' with the Lord," and this was in fact what I called the piece for many years. His alternative title suggestion was "Chattin' with the Big Guy." On page 37 of the original manuscript, Dad had God pettishly insist on being called "Big Guy," which I thought was funny.
>
> Dad started chapters in *What Dreams May Come* with "teasers," provocative and intriguing little pieces from the upcoming chapter, meant to pique the readers' interest. He suggested I do the same thing here, then went through and picked out some possibilities. Some of his suggestions are hilarious: "Come ye back as a porta-potty, fool!"; "Is there, like, an afterlife for cats?"; "Some souls return as buildings, Lord?"
>
> On page 5 Dad had Gordon ask the Father, "Why do you say 'ye?'" The Father's response: "Just a habit." On page 8 Dad made a follow-up joke: Gordon asks, "Why do you say 'verily,' the Father?" "Just another habit." Then on page 13, Dad finished off the joke: "Why do you say 'yea yea' and speak backwards?" Gordon asks. "It's a habit, get over it!" (On page 16, when the Father uses "verily," Dad added

a quick, defensive, "Don't ask me about 'verily' again!")

In my original version of the story, the president who came back from the dead was John F. Kennedy, not Abraham Lincoln. "I think JFK is too horrible," Dad wrote on page 29, and he was right, it was.

On page 34, Dad suggested that I change the main character's name from "Gordon Whitehead" to "Gordon Blackhead," which may actually be a funnier name.

Then, at the end, my favorite of Dad's jokes: I had the Father, about to depart, say "Bye" to Gordon. Dad changed the line to "*Ciao*." I thought God breaking into Italian for no reason whatsoever was wonderfully ludicrous.

7

It would be nice to report that the positive experience Dad and I had discussing "Mondays with the Lord" helped heal our relationship, that before long we were able to get back to pleasant and happy interactions, watching Dodgers games, talking about movies, and laughing together. It would be nice, but it would also be false. The truth is, before long Dad and I were arguing again, and we continued doing so pretty much all the way to the end.

Four final memories:

1. July 2012. Dad's eighty-six and in failing health; he has less than a year to live. My wife Trish and I, along with our kids William and Kate, are visiting with Mom and Dad. We're in their backyard. We're chatting about the past, and it comes up that my sister Alison and I had shared a bedroom when we were both little. Mom instantly protests.

   "You did not share a bedroom, Chris."

   "We did, Mom. Dad, you remember, right?"

   Dad starts to chuckle, he has a sense of where this

thing is going, of Mom's semi-absurdist thinking. "They definitely shared a bedroom, honey."

"Oh no, I would never have put you two in the same room."

"Well, you did, Mom, because we did share a room, for several years, in fact."

"No way. Impossible," she protests. Dad is laughing now.

"Where did I sleep then, Mom?"

"Well, not with Ali!"

Dad, through his laughter: "They did share a bedroom, honey. Chris is right."

Mom hesitates, considers. ". . . *Did* they?"

Dad nods firmly. "Yes, honey, they definitely did."

"Hmmmph," Mom says. Then, after a long and kind of perfectly timed beat: "Well, I still don't think you did." And with that Dad collapses in laughter, practically falls out of his chair, his whole body shakes, tears stream down his face. The man loved to laugh to the end.

2. November 6, 2012, Election Day in the United States, the day Barack Obama is reelected as president. I've flown down to LA to see Mom because her heart is faltering. She's at a doctor's appointment, so it's just me and Dad in the house. We're sitting in the family room. Dad's in his rocking chair.

   Dad tells me about an idea he has for a new movie version of *The Shrinking Man* that he's working on with my brother. After so many years, he's had a realization, he says. At the end of the story, Dad tells me, when Scott Carey shrinks into the atomic world, he's actually shrinking into heaven. "He shrinks into *heaven*?" I remember asking. "Yeah, heaven—what do you think?" "I'm not sure I understand the logic of it, to be honest, Dad." "What do you mean?" "I mean, why would one shrink into heaven?" Dad shakes his head, annoyed, "You don't get it."

A few minutes later I take Dad's hand. It's quiet, close. "How are you doing, Pop?" I ask.

He gazes into space, silent for a long moment before he says, "I feel hollow."

I say nothing, unsure how to respond. Dad pauses, stares ahead. "I've never been close to anyone. I don't understand other people, I never have."

I look at him, wondering if he'll turn to me and say, "What happened to us, Chris?" and we'll have one last chance to reconnect. But he just stares forward, lost in his own thoughts.

Later that night though, as I pass by Mom and Dad's bedroom (I'm staying over, sleeping in the front room), Dad calls out to me in a thin, reedy voice. I can't hear what he's said so I stop. He's sitting up in bed, looking at me. "Did you say something, Pop?" "I said I still love you." "I still love you too," I reply.

These "I love yous" are the last ones ever spoken, on either side. At the time, I wasn't sure I believed either one of them was true.

3. June 2013. Dad's in the hospital now, days away from death. I've flown down to LA to see him one last time, say goodbye. I enter his hospital room. No one else is there. They've all left to give me a moment alone with Dad. He glances over at me. "Oh, it's my other son," he says. My brother has been doing most of Dad's emotional caretaking for many years now. I've done very little. I moved a thousand miles away, that's certainly part of it, but it's more than that. I've held back, not wanted to do much. And Dad's annoyed with me for that. I sit down and we look at each other. I take Dad's hand.

   "How you doin', Dad?"

   "Okay . . . you know . . . tired . . ."

   "Sure."

   "How are the kids?"

   They're good, I tell him, following up with a bit of information about what Will and Kate are up to. Dad nods vaguely, "That's good." More silence.

   "Oh, I saw the *Somewhere in Time* musical," I tell Dad, referring to a theatrical version of his time-travel book that has recently premiered in Portland. He perks up. "How was it?" "Pretty good," I lie. "You'll like it when you and Mom come up." The plan is for him and Mom to fly up and all of us to see the show together, something that is obviously not going to happen. "It's going to Broadway, you know," he says. "I know, that's great."

   Silence again, this time for several minutes.

Finally, I start to get up. "I guess I'll let someone else talk to you now, Dad."

"Okay."

"It was good to see you."

"Yeah, you too, Chris."

"Bye."

"Bye." And I walk out of the room.

A week later Dad was dead.

I had wondered beforehand if I was going to cry when it happened. I honestly wasn't sure. Dad and I had been close for a very long time, but we'd also been distant, even estranged, for a very long time. Days passed . . . then weeks . . . and I didn't shed a single tear. I felt weird about it, like there was something wrong with me.

4. Late October 2013, four months after Dad's death. Our twelve-year-old Labrador retriever, Clark, got sick and over the space of two days died. As Clark lay on our spare bedroom floor, not eating or drinking, slowly fading away, I spent a lot of time with him, lying next to him, stroking his head and body, talking to him. Clark was an odd dog—a big, ungainly, and frankly strange animal who'd lived on the streets for awhile as a puppy and was consequently extremely nervous and anxious. The kids sometimes compared him to the mainly good-natured but occasionally "aggro" Patrick Starfish on *SpongeBob SquarePants*. I didn't love Clark that much is I guess what I'm saying. We've definitely had dogs I loved more

(thinking of you, Roxy and Violet). But as I lay next to him on the wood floor, petting him and holding him, I found myself shuddering with tears at times, my voice catching as I told Clark over and over how very much I loved him, how happy I was that I'd known him, how terribly I'd miss him when he was gone.

If I'm right, Dad and I won't ever see each other again. All that's left is my memories of him, and when I die those will be gone too. June 2013 was the end of our story and there will be no more.

If Dad's right, on the other hand, and we DO see each other again in the afterlife, well, I think that'd be lovely. We'll talk about the Dodgers, of course (Dad will be delighted that they finally won the World Series again), as well as comedy and movies and our many happy memories. It'll be great. For a day or two.

If we have "eternity," on the other hand? Honestly, it's pretty likely that before long we'll be arguing about the afterlife in the afterlife. And I'd like to think—and you know, I actually do think—that we'll laugh about that.

So long, Pop. Thanks for everything.

CONVERSATIONS
WITH THE FATHER

CONVERSATIONS WITH THE FATHER

GORDON WHITEHEAD

Inner Truth Press
Simi Valley, California

To my Father,
in so many ways the coauthor of this particular story.

INTRODUCTION

Congratulations, blessed friend, for you now hold in your hands a book of tremendous, life-changing significance.

You have come to this book because you are searching. How do I know this? Because I too was searching, frankly lost, when this remarkable and profound document was born.

Looking back on that time (was it less than a year ago? it seems like much longer), I am struck by how deeply confused and troubled I was. I was newly separated from my wife. My relationship with our eleven-year-old son was strained, at best. I was working on, to be honest, struggling with a novel. I was eating too much, exercising too little, watching too much TV. All in all, not a happy man.

Then, one drizzly March morning, as I sat at my computer, staring at the screen, attempting to work out a story point . . . how to even say this? In a moment, everything changed.

The scene I was trying to write, the climactic showdown between the hero and villain of my story, was not coming together the way I wanted it to. "Dammit," I remember thinking to myself, "why can't I get this thing to work?" I then remember looking up from the computer, gazing around my

dark, barely unpacked apartment and asking myself, "Why can't I get *anything* to work?"

And that's when the miracle happened.

FIRST CONVERSATION

Suddenly I typed something. But no, that's not quite right. "I" didn't type anything; instead, it was as if my fingers were possessed as they tapped the keyboard. It was startling, unlike anything I'd ever felt, not frightening exactly, but unsettling. Then, looking at the screen, my breath caught.

I can tell you if you'd like, it read.

I stared at the words, motionless. Then, before I could do anything more, once again my fingers were flying across the keyboard. *I said I can tell you why things are not working out for you if you'd like to know, Gordon.*

I swallowed, hesitated for a long moment, then finally typed: Who exactly are you?

The response came quickly. *Do you not know?*

No, I typed. I have no idea what the hell is even happening here.

I think you do.

What, are you my subconscious or something?

If you wish to think of me in this way, of course you can. Yet I tell you I am something more, much more than that.

I'm obviously talking to myself here. I have to stop.

Of course you are talking to yourself, my child. That is how one speaks to me.

How am I your child?

Everyone is my child, Gordon.

What, now you're saying you're God??

This I have been called, yes. Also Allah, Krishna, Zeus, Thor, and many, many other names. Yet I prefer to be known simply as "The Father."

Okay, this is nuts.

At that point the keys moved in a sudden, intense, almost angry flurry: *Question not my existence, child, nor whether I am here speaking to you, for I tell you that I AM.*

Why the hell would God be talking to me?

Is the answer to this question not obvious, my child?

No, not at all!

It is because you need me.

And you're here to, what, help me?

If you will allow me to, yes.

And how exactly are you going to help me, "God"?

I will start by teaching you about IT, child.

What is IT?

Inner Truth. You proclaim that outer things are "not working," yet I tell you that you need these outer things only because you are lacking IT. Think your outer things would matter at all if your Inner Truth was being served?

I literally have no idea, I've literally never thought about any of these things before.

I tell you most forcefully that outer things would not matter.

IT is what matters, my child, IT and only IT.

Inner Truth.

Precisely, Inner Truth. And as IT increases, what is NOT—Needing Outer Things—becomes unimportant.

So you're basically saying that all my problems pertain to Inner Truth?

Yours and everyone else's, yes, of course.

So it's the same problem with Joan . . . Brent . . . my book, everything?

IT is all that matters.

Fine. Let's play this out, "God." If "IT" is the most important thing in life, then why have I lost contact with it?

Because you have been blinded by other things, child, outer things, let us call them "Items": Inner Truth Easily Missed.

And you're saying that "Items" are bad?

There is no "good" or "bad" as you currently think of them, child. What I am saying is this: It is not in "Items" that you will find meaning in life, but rather in IT.

So you're saying that if I want my life to work better, I need to work on Inner Truth.

This is precisely what I am saying.

I mean, it's not terrible advice I seem to be giving myself here. It is definitely weird that I'm doing it as supposedly the creator of the entire universe.

I am not merely the creator of your universe, my child.

What do you mean by that?

Think ye I am only large enough to create one universe?

Well, this is the only universe we know of, right? And

seriously . . . ye?

I tell ye there is a vast multitude of other universes.

Okay, I'll bite. How many other universes are we talking about?

Behind the number one, place a line of zeros stretching from New York City to Los Angeles.

Okay . . .

Then multiply that number by one hundred trillion.

That's an incredibly huge number.

To you it is huge perhaps. To me, it simply is.

As long as I'm having this bizarre dialogue with myself, I might as well ask something that I've often wondered about, "God."

Proceed, child.

Which religion is true?

I tell you none of them are true yet simultaneously all of them are true.

Can you please explain that?

No religion sees me exactly as I am, yet each of them sees some aspect of me. Collectively, they come close to perceiving me; individually they are pieces of a puzzle, meaningless without the other pieces.

You know, that actually makes a lot of sense. And as long as we're here—was Jesus actually your son?

He was. Exactly as the Buddha, Confucius, and Muhammad were. Not to mention Gandhi, Martin Luther King, William Shakespeare, Johann Sebastian Bach, and many others. Even now, I tell you, there are several such "children" of mine wandering

among you.

Like who?

Bruce Springsteen would be one.

Wait, Springsteen??

I tell you that Bruce Springsteen's music brings forth my greatest truth.

I mean, I've always loved Bruce, I've seen him in concert like ten times, but I never thought that a rock star—

Do not limit your thinking, my child.

Who else is a child of yours?

Comedian Jerry Seinfeld.

Seriously?

Surprised, are you?

Well yeah!

You should not be for laughter is a precious gift I have bestowed upon my children and I tell you most forcefully that Jerry Seinfeld is the funniest man in the world!

I loved his show.

Deeply does Jerry Seinfeld explore the mysteries and absurdities of human existence and always does Jerry Seinfeld find something witty in it!

He's incredibly clever.

Never have I created a more clever mind than that of Jerry Seinfeld!

And will there be more children of yours in the future?

Of course there will. A being known as FL-241-X will at some point be a beloved child of mine.

"FL-241-X"? Is that, like, a robot name?

Think ye that humans are the end of the story, my child?

I mean quite honestly, I've never thought about any of this before.

I tell you humans are NOT the end of the story.

So what does that mean? That robots will replace us?

It does.

And is that going to happen, you know, soon?

Let me put it this way, Gordon: Your grandson Maurice will be a heroic soldier in the Great Robot War.

So you're saying this is going to happen in, like, twenty-five years?

I do not argue with your mathematical calculations.

If that was actually true, shouldn't I, like, tell the world or something?

The world would not listen to you, child. The world will find out in good time when the robots attack. Rest assured, however, in the comforting certainty that your grandson Maurice will be a great hero.

Maurice is a weird name to give a kid.

It will be your suggestion, child.

That's odd because I don't even much like it.

And now, dear one, as I have many other children to attend to, I must depart.

Wait, now you're going?

Stay true to IT, child.

But wait . . . Hello? . . . Hello??

As suddenly as it had come, however, the presence was gone. I sat there in silence for a long moment, staring at

the screen in disbelief at what had just happened. It was . . . unthinkable. Of course I instantly understood what had occurred: I had been upset and started talking to myself, that was the only thing that made any sense. I didn't believe in "spirits," I wasn't and never had been "religious," I'd always considered myself a skeptic, in fact. There was no way I was going to believe that some spiritual entity, not to mention the creator of the entire universe (or, I suppose, multiverse, according to him) had come and started talking to me.

But as I slowly read back over the words on the computer screen, the truth was that I had no idea what to make of them. The way this presence had expressed itself did not sound remotely like me. The presence had numerous theories and opinions that had literally never even occurred to me. In some strange way, as I studied the screen, I could not escape the feeling that these words I was reading were not mine.

The question was then, whose words were they?

SECOND CONVERSATION

The next day the presence returned.

Greetings, child.

You're back.

How are you today, dear one?

Honestly, I've been better.

Tell me.

The truth is, I slept terribly. Joan told me last night she doesn't see me moving home anytime soon. Then this morning, Brent wouldn't even get on the phone with me. Also, as of an hour ago, my book is still not working. So I mean, in terms of "Inner Truth" solving everything, what gives, right?

Indeed, child, what does give? Certainly not you.

What do you mean by that?

You think you can reflect upon Inner Truth for one single evening and everything in your life will instantly change for the better?

I thought—

You thought I was giving you a destination: I was not. I was providing you with a path. A path which you have just now taken the very first steps upon. A path which is, as you will soon discover

if you have the courage to stay upon it, both long and arduous.

I guess I didn't understand.

Seek rather to over-stand, child. Seek rather to sideways-stand, behind-stand, before-stand; seek rather to stand in as many places as you possibly can so that when you do stand, you stand not under, but rather under-stand, do you see?

I mean . . . I'm not sure . . .

You must understand first of all, Gordon, that things are not always as they seem. Sometimes, I tell you, that which you call "right" is actually "wrong" while that which you call "wrong" is in fact "right."

If that's true, then what happens to morality?

Morality is nothing more than a concept which humans have laid on top of existence, a template, at best.

Okay, but in terms of right and wrong, what about murder, isn't that wrong?

All those who are murdered, I repeat, ALL, have chosen to be murdered.

Why would someone choose to be murdered?

Perhaps in a previous existence, they murdered someone themselves. Perhaps they are seeking redemption. Or perhaps they simply enjoy being murdered.

Okay, I don't understand that at all.

Have you not heard of "masochism," my child?

Sure, but not of people who actually like to be murdered.

Yet I tell you they exist.

But—

"But" is simply "Barely Understood Thoughts," Gordon. That

which you do not immediately understand, you dismiss with "but, but, but."

Sure . . .

A certain number of what you call "murders" are necessary for my cosmic balance to be maintained and fortunately there are those who do enjoy being murdered.

That's incredibly weird. But what about when bad things happen to children? That's got to be wrong, right?

You may find the following concept difficult to grasp, child.

Try me.

When a child is harmed, what is hurt is simply a body, not a soul.

And why is that?

Because until the soul enters the child's body, which happens later than you might think, all that is being harmed is a physical vehicle, an "empty boat," as it were.

At what age does the soul enter the child's body?

Ten.

Wait, ten??

You have heard me correctly, child.

But—

Notice that I am not saying that it is "good" to harm a child, for I tell you most forcefully that it is not.

But you are saying that children are . . . ?

Empty boats, yes.

Until they're ten years old.

Or thereabouts, yes.

Okay, what about when bad things happen to eleven-

year-olds then?

They chose it.

So you mean, if Brent got hit by a car tomorrow . . . ?

He would have chosen it, yes.

But I mean . . . why??

Sometimes to escape earthly pain; sometimes to pay a karmic debt; most often, to be near ME.

In what, "heaven"?

If you wish to call it that, yes.

I have to say, I don't understand the logic of this system at ALL. Why would the soul enter the body so late?

Understand that there are only a limited number of what you would call "souls," child. At any given time each of these "souls" is required to inhabit a number of different vehicles, sometimes as many as fifty or a hundred. Because inhabiting a vehicle involves a great deal of work for these souls, I decided to focus their "soul-energy" on human beings between the ages of ten and seventy.

Wait, now you're saying that people over seventy have no soul either?

In general, they do not.

So, you mean, my parents . . . ?

There is nobody home.

No . . . That's not possible.

Have you not noticed the change in your parents over the past five years, Gordon?

I mean, sure, maybe a little but I assumed that was just them aging.

No. Their souls have departed and they are empty boats.

They are definitely different.

Indeed they are, because there is nobody home.

When you said each soul sort of "inhabits" a number of different vehicles?

Yes.

Does that mean that my soul is in other "vehicles" at this very moment?

Of course it does. Your soul presently inhabits forty-two other bodies, to be precise.

Wow! And do I know any of these other me's?

You have perhaps heard of one of them . . .

Who?

I cannot reveal the vehicle's name, child. I can, however, give you a small clue. "BFJS."

Wait . . . Is that Bruce Frederick Joseph Springsteen?

It is.

Bruce and I share the same soul?? Is that why I love his music so much?

Yea, for verily "his" music is "your" music.

I always felt that in some way! I always thought I was crazy for thinking it!

"Crazy" you most certainly were not, dear one.

So, like, if I ever met Bruce, would we know we were parts of the same soul?

Perhaps not consciously, but on some unspoken level, yes. These meetings between what one might in a certain sense call "soulmates" often lead to deep and instantaneous connection, two parts of the same soul celebrating in the pure joy and exaltation of Re-Union.

This is a weird question to ask . . .

The best questions often are, my child.

Are Joan and I "soulmates?"

What think you, Gordon?

I mean, I think we are. I definitely hope we are . . . but sometimes I have to wonder. The truth is, she doesn't even seem to like me anymore.

You wish for Joan to be like "you," child, but Joan is not like "you," Joan is like "Joan," only "you" are like "you."

Right, I get that.

Only you possess your essential "You-ness."

My essential "Me-ness?"

No, your essential "You-ness." Your essential "Me-ness" is the healthier part of your being, the part that thinks, "Yes. I am Me." Your essential "You-ness," on the other hand, seeks love in others.

Is that to say that I need more "Me-ness" and less "You-ness?"

You-ness is not bad per se, but yes, Me-ness is better. Better still, however, much better, is "I-ness."

"I-ness?"

I-ness is that most inner part of you, child, the part that feels your deepest hopes, fears, and desires.

What's the difference between "Me-ness" and "I-ness"?

What's the difference between a rain puddle and the sea? Between a gnat and an elephant? Between a grain of sand and Mount Everest?

So a huge difference.

A vast difference.

I really do want Joan back.

I know that you do, my son.

I miss her so much, I feel so empty without her. And the thing that kills me is I have no idea how to win her back, like, what could I even do at this point?

The answer to this question is obvious, child.

. . . Inner Truth?

Exactly. Ask yourself, child: How can you make manifest Joan's Inner Truth?

How can I . . . ?

I will pose the question another way: What is Joan's IT?

You know, she likes to travel, she likes a nice meal, gardening . . .

You are missing the point completely, child. Think more deeply: What is Joan's IT?

. . . I guess I don't exactly know.

I will give you a hint then. It starts with "S" and ends in "E-X."

Wait, sex?

Surprised, are you?

I mean, Joan likes sex, definitely, but I don't think it's her IT.

You are mistaken. It is. IT is.

Even if it was, she doesn't want to have sex with me, she's made that abundantly clear.

It is not merely "sex" that Joan wants, child.

What else is it?

Joan wishes to be SEEN AND APPRECIATED.

Right, and that means . . . what?

Is it not obvious that Joan wants to be photographed having sex, child?

Wait, what?

Joan's Inner Truth is to be DESIRED. This, I tell ye, is what ye must manifest for her.

So you're saying I should, like, take pictures of us having sex?

Exactly. Then post them on the internet.

What?

You heard me.

I can pretty much guarantee that Joan doesn't want sex photos on the internet.

You are mistaken. She does.

I'd love it if she did, it's definitely something that I've thought about, you know, like a fantasy or whatever . . .

It is not fantasy, it is truth and you must now act upon it, Gordon Whitehead!

But—

"Barely Understood Thoughts" again! You ask for answers, child, yet when I give them to you, you do not listen.

I'm just saying—

What I am offering you here is not a "suggestion," Gordon, it is a command. Ye SHALL photograph Joan during sex and ye SHALL post the resulting photos on the internet!

The problem is—

You are mulish and hard to reach at times, child.

I'm sorry, I just—

It is time for you to call me The Father.

Wait, seriously?

You need to call me The Father NOW.

This feels incredibly weird.

You are resisting me, child, and it is time for you to stop doing so.

But—

Or would you prefer that I prove to thee my powers by striking thee dead?

Okay, don't do that.

Because I could, you know. I literally do it all the time.

Right, I don't want that.

I could make your heart stop right this second or make a blood vessel in your brain pop or cause your intestines to suddenly explode, would you like that, Gordon?

I definitely wouldn't.

Then call me The Father.

Fine . . . The Father.

Say it again.

The Father.

Once more.

The Father!

That is excellent.

Can I ask you a question, though?

You may.

How am I supposed to actually do this? I mean, just practically speaking, Joan does not want to have sex with me.

I tell you she does.

Well, she says she doesn't.

She is not being truthful.

Okay, but—

Bring two bottles of wine when you see her.

That'll help, I guess, but then, even if I do get her to have sex with me, how exactly am I supposed to get photos of it?

When Joan is in the bathroom you must rig a hidden camera, my child.

Wouldn't that be, I don't know . . . unscrupulous?

When you are helping another person find their Inner Truth, I tell you there is no such thing as "unscrupulous," child.

So it's okay to basically trick her then?

In the same way that on Halloween your children say "Trick or treat"; with this "Trick," you will give Joan the "Treat" of IT.

Okay then, I guess I'll do it. I mean, I'll at least try.

Splendid, my child. Go give IT to Joan.

THIRD CONVERSATION

How are you today, my son?

Not great, The Father.

No?

I have to tell you, the photographing thing didn't go well at all.

This is your perception, my child.

No, I mean, it really didn't.

Tell me.

I did, amazingly, manage to get Joan into bed and I also managed to rig a hidden camera in our bedroom and take some pictures, a couple of which turned out pretty well, I think—

I agree with you, they did.

What, you've seen them?

All that you have seen, I have seen.

Okay, wow.

More than that, I tell you, all that you have experienced, I have experienced.

Are you saying you've had sex, The Father?

Indeed I have. Many times.

This is a weird question but with who?

It would not be very "godly" of me to name names, now would it, child?

I guess not.

I will say only this much: Her initials are M.M.

Wait, Marilyn Monroe?

You said it, not me.

But is that right?

Yes.

Marilyn Monroe was amazing.

All of my creations are "amazing" to me, child—but I get your point, Marilyn was and still is amazing.

You're still having sex with Marilyn Monroe now?

Yes.

That's incredible—but can we get back to me and Joan?

Several of the photos are quite attractive, child, notably the ones where Joan is on top.

Yeah, those are definitely the best ones, they're the ones I posted on this website called Hotwives. I put eight pictures on there while Joan was in the bathroom afterwards and then when she came out I told her I had something to show her and then . . . well, I showed her.

And how did she react?

Honestly, she went totally ballistic on me. She was enraged, like way more so than I've ever seen her.

Or at least pretending to be.

I don't think she was pretending.

Hard it is for Joan to admit her Inner Truth, greatly must she

protest it. Yet I tell you this, my son: Joan is delighted in her soul to have those pictures on Hotwives.

She actually threatened to sue me, The Father.

That is just talk.

Still—

She will not sue you, child, for that would only call more attention to the photos.

I guess so, but . . .

It may take Joan time, child, for she is not fully in touch with her own IT, but eventually she will come to see what you have given her as a great gift.

I tried to make things better with her afterwards, sort of explain things by reading one of our conversations to her, but she said I was just making it all up.

She is mistaken in this belief.

She said I was obviously talking to myself. I told her I thought the exact same thing at first but had come to see it differently.

Joan's eyes are on the ground, my son, not the sky.

She told me I was full of shit, The Father, excuse my language.

I am not offended by the word "shit," child. Verily I tell ye that another word for "shit" is "fertilizer," thus when Joan told you that you were "full of shit," what she was actually telling you was that you were "full of fertilizer," which all living things, yea I say ALL, need to grow.

I don't think that's how she meant it.

When our communication is complete, you will share the entire

dialogue with Joan, child. Until that time, do not speak of it to her anymore.

I shouldn't try convincing her?

Believe you, will she?

No way.

This then is your answer, is it not?

I guess so, but it saddens me.

Your sadness speaks well of you, my son.

I have to ask you about something else, The Father.

Proceed, my child.

I stopped by my parents today and I have to admit, I see what you were saying about them being different, they definitely are.

They are empty boats, child.

I felt that and it seemed, like, super-sad, it made me feel like, I don't know, maybe their deaths are not that far off?

This I cannot tell you.

I'm definitely not one of those people who thinks about an inheritance, The Father.

I know that you are not, Gordon.

It's not like that, not at all. I just think that seeing them that way kind of freaked me out because it made me feel like, I don't know, I'm next.

That is correct, child. You are.

And that made me start to wonder, what *does* actually happen when we die? Is it, whatever, "the end"?

Think ye I would create souls simply to destroy them after what, to me, is the blink of an eye, child? Of course it is not the

end. There is more, MUCH more.

Do you mean, like, reincarnation?

Reincarnation is part of the story, of course. Depending on how one has lived, one might come back as a king or a mosquito, as well as anything in between. One might even—and this will, I think, surprise you, child—come back as a building.

Wait, one can get reincarnated as a building??

Familiar, are you, with the Space Needle in Seattle, Washington, my son?

Sure!

That is Eleanor Roosevelt.

Wow!

The Sydney Opera House is rock-and-roll legend The Big Bopper.

Damn!

And Yankee Stadium? Marcel Proust!

That's . . . not what I would have expected.

What you refer to as "the end" is not, in many cases, the end at all.

What do you mean by that, The Father?

What I mean, quite simply, is that people sometimes come back from the dead.

They do??

Verily.

I thought the only person who'd ever returned from the dead was Jesus, and some people weren't even sure about him.

Jesus did return from the dead, and so have many others.

Who else came back, The Father?

Four days after he was killed, President Abraham Lincoln returned from the dead.

How come no one saw him?

He was, unfortunately, locked in a wooden coffin.

Abraham Lincoln came back from the dead just to be locked inside his wooden coffin?

Sadly, yes.

But that's awful.

Not so awful as you might think, child. Honest Abe used the time meaningfully, making the best of a bad situation.

What did he do?

He sang, told himself jokes, did some light calisthenics.

Who else came back from the dead, The Father?

Familiar are ye with baseball slugger Willie Stargell?

Sure, he played for the Pirates, he was great.

Willie Stargell rose from the dead not long after his passing.

What did he do?

He sat up, watched a bit of TV, had a sip of water, then laid back down and essentially "re-died."

I'm sorry, but I don't understand this, The Father. What's the point of Willie Stargell coming back from the dead just to watch a little bit of TV?

TV was all that was available to him, my child. If there had been a baseball game he might well have played in it.

Could he have done well, The Father?

No, dear one, Willie Stargell would have struck out on three pitches, so it is just as well that he did not play.

I suppose he could have drawn a walk.

Hear me now and hear me well: Any pitcher who cannot throw three strikes to a dead man does not deserve to be a major leaguer!

Could the pitcher have thrown a wild pitch and hit Willie Stargell and put him on base that way?

That is indeed possible, yes.

And if the pitcher had then balked, Willie Stargell would have gone to second base, right, The Father?

Yes, but I tell you he would have gone no further, for he would then have surely been picked off!

What if the next batter had hit a home run on the first pitch, The Father?

Then Willie Stargell would have scored a run but enough speculation about Willie Stargell, the truth is none of these things actually happened.

My parents are planning on getting cremated after they die, The Father. What do you think about that?

I tell you that cremation is a grave mistake, child. Many people there are, yea many, who have returned from the dead just in time to get burned to a crisp in a crematorium.

That's awful!

Indeed it is. Organ donations, likewise, while of noble intent, are equally misguided. One woman, a grandmother of six, returned from the dead only to stagger blindly around her hospital room and finally topple out a window to her "re-death," simply because her eyes had just been removed.

Given these terrible possibilities, what should I do with my parents' bodies when they pass, The Father?

This is an excellent question, Gordon, and I shall hold forth upon it. First, place the body in a bed, dressing it in comfortable and loose-fitting clothes. Play quiet, mellow music; Steely Dan is always a good choice. Place a glass of water near the body, along with a washbasin to "freshen up." Know that if your loved one does return, it will only be for a short time. Before long, they will inevitably "re-die." View their return, thus, as a wonderful opportunity for one final chance to tie up loose ends, or share happy memories. Quiet activities will not be a problem for most returnees: Low-key board games, reading, and jigsaw puzzles are all good. Avoid strenuous or taxing activities, however: No biking, tennis, or inline skating, for instance. Returnees will need very little, if any, sleep. (Though there is a small minority of them who will sleep through their entire return.) Most returnees will not be hungry, but if they are, providing a light snack is thoughtful: Sliced fruit, nuts, crackers, and cheese are excellent. Avoid potato pancakes, falafel, and all kinds of chowders. Avoid also liquor, as tolerance for alcohol will be extremely low. If a returnee does drink they may quickly become agitated, paranoid, even belligerent. If this occurs, speak calmly to them, try to get them to lay down and watch some TV. If they persist in their belligerence, it may be necessary to restrain or even, in the worst cases, "re-kill" them. If you need to re-kill a returnee, gently place a pillow over their face and smother them for 10–15 minutes. If this does not work, place the pillowcase over the returnee's head and "beat them to death" with a baseball bat. This will kill all but the hardiest returnees, who may in extremely rare cases need to be beheaded. Only decapitate a returnee if it is absolutely necessary. Speak calmly and gently as

you approach the returnee, perhaps complimenting them on their looks or offering them a cup of tea. Then, when you get close enough, chainsaw their head off.

What if you don't have a chainsaw, The Father?

Then the task will be far more difficult, child, yet I tell you it must be done.

It's weird but I still can't get over the thing with Abraham Lincoln.

Yes, it was quite disturbing.

To get shot the way he did and then come back to life only to be locked in your coffin . . . it's like a nightmare.

Seeing Honest Abe try to claw his way out of that wooden coffin and listening to him scream in terror is something I will never forget, my child.

Couldn't you have just let him out, The Father?

It does not work that way, child. I wish that it did, for I certainly would have.

How long did Abraham Lincoln have to endure it?

Not long.

That's good.

Two or three weeks, at most.

That seems like a really long time.

All time is relative. What is ultimately the saddest thing is this: Had President Lincoln not been shot, I tell you that he would have lived for a very, yea very, long time.

How long?

Abraham Lincoln would have lived to be three hundred years old, my child.

Three hundred?! But no one has ever lived that long!

Trees live that long, as do giant sea turtles.

Sure, but I mean, no human.

This is because no human has ever properly taken care of themselves, child. If they did, I tell you they could easily live to be three hundred years old.

I'd love to live to be three hundred years old!

And so you could, dear one.

What would I need to do to live that long, The Father?

You would need to live a "Wholesome" rather than a "Hole-some" life, child.

What do you mean by "Hole-some"?

Thinking of nothing but pleasing your Holes.

That's fairly harsh.

Think ye it's untrue, my son?

I mean . . . I guess not, but—

If you wish to live to be three hundred years old, you need to stop filling your mouth-hole with french fries and ice cream sundaes and jellybeans and fill it instead with healthy grains and legumes. You need to fill your nose-holes not with perfumed cleaning products and fancy colognes but rather with fresh flowers and delightful sachets of potpourri. You need to fill your eye-holes not with flashy movies or violent video games but rather with the glory of sunsets at the beach or the beauty of senior citizens' smiling, wrinkled faces. You need to fill your ear-holes not with harsh, ugly metal "music" but rather with the warm and earnest tones of Bruce Springsteen or the clever artistry of Steely Dan. Most importantly, child, yea, most importantly by far, you need to fill your sex and

elimination-holes with Love rather than with Lust.

. . . That's a lot to think about, The Father.

The Truth always is, my child. Think about that until we meet again.

FOURTH CONVERSATION

Can I say something that's been bothering me, The Father?

Of course, dear one.

I've been feeling somehow *unworthy* of all this attention you've been paying me.

There is no need for that, child.

No?

Think ye I would have come to thee if I found thee "unworthy," Gordon?

I guess not.

You need not "guess," dear one, for I tell you most forcefully that I would not have. Surprise you, would it, if I told you that I had great respect for you, my son?

For me, The Father?

Indeed.

But . . . why?

Think ye there are many who would be willing to do what you are doing here?

I . . . don't know.

Many there are, child, I tell you many, who would feel like a complete fool for doing what you are doing.

I mean . . . I guess that's true.

"Look at the fool sitting at his computer, pretending he's communicating with God," they would laugh.

Right . . .

Yet I say unto you: They are the Fools, "Finding Only Outer Love."

That's a good acronym, The Father.

In the end these Fools will have nothing and their scornful laughs will stick in their throats as they are turned into mosquitoes in their next lives.

Or maybe buildings, The Father?

Indeed. "Come ye back as a porta-potty, fool."

"Find your Inner Truth now, fool."

"I can't, it's covered in poop." Ahahahahahahahahahahahaha!!

Ahahahahahahahahahahahahahahahahaha!

Ahahahahahahahahahahahahahahahahaha!

Ahahahahahahahahahahahahahahahahahahaha! I'm dying here, The Father!

Yea, this is very hilarious!

But I'm wondering . . . ?

Yes, my son?

Should I, like, cut this part out of the book? I'm a little worried that some people might find it, you know . . .

"Blasphemous," child?

Well . . . yeah.

Think ye that I must always be "serious," my child?

No no.

Am I not allowed to make a joke, even an "irreverent" one?

No, of course you are, I just meant–

That you are not sure the world is ready for a God this free-wheeling and humorous?

Yes.

Hear me now, Gordon Whitehead, and hear me well: I am ALL. Just as I am in every prayer and poem and painting, so too am I in every raunchy joke and ugly epithet. I am not only "beauty," child, I am also what you would call "ugliness." Just as I am in every birth, so too I am in every death. I am in every bluebird that topples from its branch, in every vole eaten by an owl, in every bug smashed upon your windshield. I am in every heart attack, every cancer, every case of lupus, shingles, and psoriasis. I am there as you battle for your life, desperately trying to fight off the bear that is eating your arm; I am there when you are swarmed by angry yellow jackets and stung to death; I am there when you eat a toxic mushroom and die in writhing agony. I am in your home, yea, in your every room. I am in your kitchen, in your refrigerator, and in your garbage disposal. I am in your bathroom, in your sink, and in your toilet. I am in your bedroom, yea, especially there, for the bedroom, I tell you, is where you come closest to knowing my deepest Inner Truth. HEAR ME, GORDON WHITEHEAD, AS I SAY IT AGAIN,IAMMMMMMMMMMMMMMMMMM MMMMMMMMMMMM.

Wow, The Father. That was just . . . extraordinary.

Concern yourself not with what feels "offensive," my child. Place all, I say ALL, of our communications in your book.

I need to ask you about something else, The Father.

Tell me, dear one.

It's not Brent's fault, obviously. Me and Joan's separation has been incredibly hard for him, I know that . . . but he's just . . . Honestly, I don't think he respects me at all, The Father.

Earned his respect, have you, child?

No, I haven't, I know I haven't! That's the problem right there, isn't it?

You already know that it is, my child.

Yes.

Yet you also know the answer to this problem, don't you?

. . . I need to help Brent find his Inner Truth, don't I, The Father?

Exactly so, my son.

The thing is I'm just not sure how to do it.

Ask yourself: What does a child need from a father?

I mean . . . someone who will protect them?

And can you think of any present situation where Brent needs your protection?

. . . In soccer maybe?

Go on.

Brent's not enjoying it. He has this coach who doesn't let him play very much.

Because?

You don't know, The Father?

I wish to hear your interpretation, child.

Because Brent's not a very good player maybe?

And why is that?

Joan thinks it's because he needs to play more.

But this coach, this Tad Gonnerd—

Wait, you know him, The Father?

I know everyone, child.

Of course, sorry.

Tad Gonnerd is a sad and stunted little man who uses his power over children to increase his pathetically low self-worth. He is small in every single way, if you catch my drift, child.

Do you mean that he has a small penis, The Father?

Tad Gonnerd has a small penis and very small balls as well. Next time around, I tell you, Tad Gonnerd will be an inchworm.

An inchworm, I get it, The Father.

Yes.

Are you suggesting that I need to stand up to Tad Gonnerd and tell him to play Brent more, The Father?

Is this not what Heroes do, my child? Stand up and protect the weak?

That's definitely true.

And when you do stand up, be assured that others will notice it, my son.

Do you mean Joan, The Father?

Joan will unquestionably notice your heroism, yes.

That would be amazing.

It will happen, dear one. Count on it.

. . . Can I say something, The Father?

What is it, my child?

It's honestly . . . it's kind of corny.

Go on, Gordon.

You're my Hero.

Thank you, child.

And I definitely needed a hero, you know? Cuz my dad definitely wasn't one, I mean even before he became an empty boat, he wasn't.

You are correct, child. He was not.

Right, and I just wanted you to know how very appreciative I am of you being my Hero.

You are more than welcome, my child. And now, as we part, I wish to leave you with this important wisdom: The only difference between "yours" and "ours" is "Y." Do you understand what I am saying?

I'm not sure I do.

"Y," Gordon. "Why."

Oh! Yes!

But the question is, "Y" is it necessary that there be any distinction between yours and ours?

I totally get that.

"Y" can't it all be "ours"?

I was just thinking the other day that if you turn the "M" in "me" over and make it into a "W" then "Me" turns into "We."

Precisely. In the same vein, if you add an "S" to "U" ("You") it becomes "Us."

That's so true!

Take that same "U," however, and add an "I" to it and what do you get?

. . . "Ui"? It's not even a word!

It's not even a word, exactly!

Why can't people "C" all these things, The Father?

Excellent, Gordon! Well done!

"G" thanks!

Haha, delightful, dear one, Jerry Seinfeld would approve! Now go forth and be Brent's Hero!

I will, The Father, I'll definitely try!!

FIFTH CONVERSATION

Sadly, my effort to be Brent's Hero could not possibly have gone worse. When I walked up to Tad Gonnerd before the next game and asked to talk to him about Brent's playing time, he glared at me with his smug little face and said, "I'm sorry but I don't have time for this right now." I wasn't about to let Gonnerd get away from me that easily though; I was determined to stand up for my son. So I tailed Gonnerd and when he kept walking away from me, I grabbed his arm and spun him around and said, "Hey man."

That's when it got bad. Gonnerd's face turned bright red and he hissed, "Do not touch me, do you understand what I'm saying? Do not touch me!" "Oh, I understand alright," I replied. "I understand that you're a defensive little man who shouldn't even be around children." Now people were gathering around us, trying to calm things down. I saw Brent with some other kids about twenty feet away. "Dad, stop it," he called out.

And maybe I should have stopped. But then Gonnerd shoved me and yelled, "Back off, man!" and, well, I lost it. I lowered my head, plowed into Gonnerd, and in seconds we

were on the ground, rolling around and fighting.

Unfortunately for me it turns out that Gonnerd wrestled in high school so I was instantly at a severe disadvantage. I got a few quick punches in, but then Gonnerd got on top of me and pinned me. I saw Brent's face in the crowd, he had tears in his eyes.

I knew I couldn't let things end like that. So when Gonnerd let me up, I grabbed for the nearest object, which happened to be a beer bottle. I swung the bottle at Gonnerd, but accidentally hit a mom, Linda Carlson, who was trying to help out, in the head. She dropped and now people were screaming at me and kids were crying and shouting. It was a complete nightmare.

The police came ten minutes later and arrested me. Joan bailed me out two hours later but wouldn't even talk to me when she drove me home and then looked at me with what felt like an awful mixture of pity and disgust when I tried to kiss her. The entire experience was deeply and horribly humiliating. Yet when I related the story to The Father, his response was startling.

Surprised would you be if I told you I was proud of you for your actions today, my son?

Proud? But why, The Father? I swung a beer bottle at someone and accidentally hit a woman in the head with it!

You did not intend to break that beer bottle on Linda Carlson's head, my child.

I truly didn't.

I know that and I forgive you for it.

Still, I feel ashamed, The Father. I feel like I made a complete idiot of myself in front of Brent. I feel like I humiliated myself.

And think ye "humiliation" is a bad thing, Gordon?

Well, it definitely feels bad.

As do the shots that protect you from getting ill, hmm?

But this is different, I mean, I did this to myself.

No, my child. I did this to you.

. . . You did, The Father?

Verily.

But . . . why?

So that you might at long last experience your own Inner Truth.

Does that mean my Inner Truth is I'm a guy who loses a fight to a much smaller man, then swings a beer bottle at him and accidentally hits some woman in the head with it?

In this case, yes, it does.

Now I feel really horrible. I mean, what could be less heroic than that?

Think ye heroes always "win," my son?

I mean—

Did Jesus "win"? Did Martin Luther King or Gandhi "win"?

I'm sorry, but I genuinely can't see putting myself in the same category as Jesus, Martin Luther King, or Gandhi, The Father.

By realizing their Inner Truths, Heroes tell us both what we are and what we are not. You have today provided Brent with a profound example of what not to be, how not to act. Do you not see

the supreme value in this?

So does that mean Brent's Inner Truth is to not be like me?

Precisely. You have released your son, freed him of the awful pressure to be like you, his Father. Brent is liberated now, able to fully be Himself. I tell you he is closer to IT at this moment than he has ever been before. Properly understood, my child, you have never done a finer thing in your life than what you did today.

I have a really hard time seeing it that way, The Father.

Without darkness, what is light, Gordon? Without hatred, what is love? Without war, what is peace?

But I don't want to be darkness, hatred, and war, The Father!

Yet you are darkness, hatred, and war, my child! And you were brave enough to allow others to see all that in you. The most loving action you could have possibly taken today was to swing that beer bottle at Tad Gonnerd's head. Consider the outcome: Brent is free, Tad Gonnerd is chastened, Linda Carlson will be fine (four stitches is not a big deal), and most importantly of all, you, my child, have been humbled.

And that's good?

Very good. For the less you think of yourself, dear one, the more that I love you.

There was another bad thing that happened today too.

Tell me, my child.

When I tried to go talk to Brent later and Joan told me to leave because he didn't want to see me, I got so upset that I backed out of the driveway too fast and accidentally ran over

Brent's cat Fitzie and killed him.

This is unfortunate, yet there is something you did not know, my child: Fitzie actually had a very large tumor in his stomach and would have been dead in less than a month.

He would have?

Indeed, and it would have been an excruciating death. In truth, therefore, you put Fitzie out of his future misery by running him over. He is in a better place now.

Sort of like a . . . cat heaven?

If you wish to call it that, yes.

What's cat heaven like anyway, The Father?

Imagine giant scratching posts, bottomless saucers of milk, and lots of mice.

Which would sort of be like a hell for the mice then, right, The Father?

Exactly so, child.

What did mice do to deserve to go to hell, though?

Who started the Black Plague?

I always thought it was rats.

All rodents, I say all rodents, shall go to hell for their role in the Black Plague! But this is not the point, child, the point is that everything you have done this day, yea, every-thing, has been both good and worthy.

Thank you, The Father, that's incredibly reassuring to hear.

Yet you do not believe it.

Well . . .

You must speak the words aloud, child.

I must . . . what—?

You must speak the words "I am a good and worthy man" aloud.

When?

Now.

. . . I find this really embarrassing, The Father.

I command ye to speak the words aloud, child! Speak now and speak LOUDLY: "I am a good and worthy man." SAY IT.

. . . I am a good and worthy man.

Louder!

I am a good and worthy man!

Louder still!

I am a good and worthy man!

LOUDER!

I AM A GOOD AND WORTHY MAN!!

AGAIN!

I AM A GOOD AND WORTHY MAN. I AM A GOOD AND WORTHY MAN! I AM A GOOD AND WORTHY MAAAAAAAAAANNNNNNNN!!!!!

Yes. Yes, my son.

Someone's pounding on the wall, The Father.

That does not matter.

"Screw you, man! I'm talking to God here!" Sorry, The Father.

As I said, it does not matter.

Hold on, The Father, I'm really sorry. "Go ahead and call the police, asshole! Yeah, you know what, blow me!" Sorry, The Father, but that guy's a complete prick, pardon my French.

I am not offended, my child, and I agree with your assessment

of him.

I don't have to leave this part in the book, do I?

Think ye the struggle with non-believers is unimportant to our story, dear one?

I mean, I guess it is important, but still—

I tell you that non-belief is an essential part of our story and must therefore remain.

Isn't me yelling about being a good and worthy man kind of bragging, The Father?

It is not bragging; it is simply an expression of your Inner Truth, child. For remember: In the absence of something, there is only Not. Yet in the absence of Not, this I tell you is where I truly reside.

In . . . Not-Not?

Yes.

But what is Not-Not?

It is not what is Not.

But . . . what isn't Not?

The question is, what ISN'T Not-Not?

. . . You know, I actually think I'm starting to understand all this stuff, The Father.

Verily you are, my child, verily you are. And I will tell you the reason why: Because you are almost ready to graduate.

. . . Graduate? What do you mean by that, The Father?

You will soon find out, beloved one, but for now, farewell.

Wait . . . The Father? Hello?

I had no idea what The Father had in mind when he used the word "graduate," but thinking that it might mean our

magnificent communications were coming to a conclusion, I knew there was one final question I had to ask him. It was a question I'd been wanting to ask for awhile but hadn't gotten up the nerve to do so. Now, with our time together potentially running out, I decided to take the plunge.

SIXTH CONVERSATION

There's something I've been wanting to ask you about for awhile now, The Father.

What is it, my child?

This is difficult but, well, here goes: I was wondering if maybe you'd be willing to read a part of my novel? I know it's a lot to ask of you, The Father, I know you're incredibly busy running the multiverse and all, but when you used the word "graduation," it made me think maybe we were nearly done and the thing is, honestly, I'd just really love to get your feedback on the book.

I would be more than happy to read your manuscript, child.

You would?

Of course I would.

That's fantastic! So I guess I'll just, like, paste it in? Would that be okay, The Father, will that work for you?

That will be perfect, child.

Great! Okay then, here goes!

At that point, I cut and pasted my novel for The Father one chapter at a time.

***

INVASION: EARTH
By Gordon Whitehead

Chapter One: “It Begins”

It was a Tuesday night. I was in the kitchen, toasting an english muffin. I’d had a long day at work and I needed a snack. I turned on the news. Same ol’. Trouble in the Mideast, somebody shot somebody else, the stock market went down, the home team won, the sun was out.

But then, at the very end, something different.

Treated almost as a joke, a story about strange lights in the night sky, unexplained but probably just the reflections of city lights or military planes. With a wink and a smile, Mr Hairdo Newsman let us know it was nothing serious. I finished my english muffin, popped some raisins into my mouth, drank a slug of o.j. and went up to bed.

In his room, Rod Jr lay sprawled on the bed, a comic book on his chest. I’m Rod Jr’s hero, partly because I’m a fireman who saves lives, I guess, but mainly because I used to be a professional baseball player. I was actually on track for a Hall of Fame career until I got beaned by Clayton Kershaw. After that, I was in a coma for three months and I never played again.

In our bedroom, my wife Maureen, all high full breasts and sleepy hair, rolled over and looked at me. “What time did Rod Jr go to bed?” I said. “Ten,” she said. “Come here.”

I stripped off my clothes and got into bed next to her. I felt her high full breasts pressing against my toned chest. Her silky hair whispered

against my cheek as she whispered huskily in my ear, "Drill me with your big tool, Rod."

I did. It was fabulous.

Afterwards, Maureen started to cry. "What is it, baby?" I murmured. "I just love you so much, Rod." "Right back atcha, sweet thing." "Let's not ever let anything change, okay?" "But baby, things do ch--"

Touching my lips, she silenced me. Her head drifted down towards my already re-growing penis. She blew me. After that we sixty-nined. I had no idea at the time that it would be the last time Maureen and I would be sixty-nining for a very, very long time.

The next day at noon, I was at Subway with my co-worker Oswald, a lean and ambitious young bug-eyed idiot. I was just finishing my chicken sandwich when the sky outside began to darken. "What's that?" Bugeyes said, looking up. "I don't know, but I definitely don't think it's good," I replied.

We rushed outside. The sky was slowly filling up with huge, silver spaceships gliding silently into place in perfect formation, hovering just above downtown Glendale, a phalanx of gleaming alienness.

A piece of lettuce hung from Bugeyes mouth as he stared upward. "What the ...?"

Then a Voice spoke.

(I was particularly excited to finally paste in chapter 23, because I knew The Father would respond favorably to it.)

Chapter 23: "Braktar Cracks"

"Destroy you, we shall, human," the Alien Leader

hissed at me. “In need of nourishment have we come to your planet, in need of large brains to eat and, small as yours turn out to be, they will simply have to suffice.”

“Fuck you, Braktar,” I spat.

“I’m sure you would like to, human, but I’m afraid this will not happen. Soon your brain will be gurgling in my belly and your body will be nothing but Dust: Dead Ugly Stupid Trash.”

“There’s just one thing you didn’t count on, Braktar. No matter how smart you Galtoids might be, no matter how big your spaceships are or how powerful your laser guns might be, we humans never EVER give up. So I have a message for you: In the end, I’m gonna watch that fat green head of yours split like an overripe watermelon hitting hot pavement!”

Braktar scowled, enraged. “Hear me now, human: You are nothing but a lowly piece of cosmic turd that I have, unfortunately, picked up on my space shoe. But shoes can be cleaned, I say, just as brains can be eaten and bodies can rot and turn into Dust, as I said, Dead Ugly Stupid Trash.”

Suddenly, I knew exactly what was bugging the Alien Leader. “I bet you have a small penis, don’t you, Braktar?” As he visibly tightened, I bored in. “That’s it, isn’t it? You’re sporting a micro-peen in your spacesuit, aren’t you? All of you Galtoids are, right? That’s why you’re so mad, cuz you have shiitake mushrooms between your legs and you can’t please the lady Galtoids, am I wrong?”

The fat-headed alien’s tentacle lashed out and slapped me wetly in the face. “Be silent!” he screamed shrilly. I smiled a tight, cool smile. “Yeah, I understand you now, Braktar. You’re not here to eat our brains, you’re here to steal our penises. Well, listen up, melon-head, it ain’t

gonna go down that way!"

My left foot slowly crept towards one of Braktar's leg-tentacles. If I could trip him, I could grab his keys, free myself from this cage in the Oval Office, get to my spaceship, and attack the alien mother-ship. But time was running out. By tomorrow the Galtoid take-over would be complete. The last human strongholds were being relentlessly attacked and the brave people hiding within them couldn't hold out much longer. I had to escape from the clutches of this alien pencil-dick and save the planet.

"You amuse me, human. Trapped in a cage you are, yet you threaten me!? Hyaaaannhh hyaaaannnhh hyaaaannhh," Braktar brayed his harsh, ugly laugh. Then pulling out a laser-weapon, he aimed it at my head. "Have you any final empty threats to make, human?"

"As a matter of fact, I do, Braktar: Have a nice trip and see you next fall!" With that, my foot suddenly shot out, caught the Alien Leader's lower tentacle, and yanked it out from under him.

As Braktar started to tumble backwards, his ugly mouth formed into a perfect "O." "Noooooooo," he screeched as his wet, vile body hit the floor. The keys to the cage flew out of his hand-tentacle and, exactly as I'd hoped, straight into the air. Quick from my years of playing ball, my hand darted out and caught the keys and within seconds I was out of the cage and gazing down at Braktar, who was now sprawled out on the Oval Office floor like a shit-faced octopus. He stared up at me, his eyes wide and frightened now. "Do not harm me, human! Do not harm me!!"

"You thought you were gonna steal our penises, Braktar, but I'll tell you what you're actually gonna get: My fist right in your fat, ugly face!"

```
With that, I punched him hard, right in the nose.
   Suddenly a bunch of Galtoid thugs sporting
laser guns burst into the Oval Office. "KILL HIM!"
Braktar screamed, tears of anger and shame filling
his eyes. The thugs started firing, but I was too
quick for them; I leapt out the window and as I
was falling, called back, "See you soon, Braktar!"
```

* * *

Thirty minutes passed. I waited nervously. Finally, unable to restrain myself any longer, I typed in, "What do you think, The Father?" There was a lengthy and frankly excruciating pause, which was followed by: *Do you really want to know, my child?* I swallowed, closed my eyes. Then I took a breath, opened my eyes and typed, "Yes, The Father, I really do."

Next came the most heartstopping words I'd ever seen in my life: *I like it very much.*

You do?!

I think it's quite promising, my son.

Do you mean it, The Father?

I do not say that which I do not mean, my child.

Right, of course not!

I think your book has marvelous potential. I found the opening scene highly effective. There was a strong sense of foreboding about what was going to happen when the spaceships arrived.

That's definitely what I was going for, The Father.

Rod is an attractive and compelling hero. And Braktar is a vivid villain.

So, like, you actually think the book's good, The Father?

I think it is very good, child. Excellent, in fact.

Was there anything about it you didn't like?

I do have a few thoughts, if you would like to hear them.

Like to hear them? Oh my god, of course I would, The Father! Yes! Please!

First of all, your choice of words is at times unnecessarily crass. The use of the term "micro-peen," for instance.

That was meant to be kind of a joke, The Father.

It is vulgar.

Right, I could change it for sure.

Also, "Drill me with your big tool, Rod." Why not "Give me your mighty manhood, Rod"?

Right, that's much better, The Father.

On another note, I am somewhat troubled by the manner of speaking you have given to Braktar.

How so, The Father?

Think ye not that Braktar's speech patterns resemble my own?

Yours, The Father? No, not at all!

I perceive that they do.

Wow, that hadn't even occurred to me.

He speaks in reverse, Braktar does, like me.

I guess, now that you mention it—

Also, Braktar uses the phrase, "Hear me now."

Which I thought was super-commanding.

It is, because it is almost exactly what I say, child!

Oh. Right.

Finally, Braktar tells Rod that soon he will be "Nothing but Dust: Dead Ugly Stupid Trash."

Yes, The Father?

This is another thing I do all the time, child; I use acronyms to make a point: It . . . But . . . Not . . . Fool.

Right, I definitely do know that, The Father, but—

Acronyms are one of my primary communication devices, Gordon, and little do I care for you using them in your story without even asking me about it! And this isn't even a good acronym. "Dead Ugly Stupid Trash"? This is witless!

I'm sorry, The Father.

"Denying Un-Scientific Truth" would be better! Or "Driving Upon Silent Trails." "Damming Up Sexual Tension" perhaps, but "Dead Ugly Stupid Trash"? This is feeble, child.

I'll definitely take that one out, The Father.

Fine. Other than these few things, as I said at the outset, I think that your story shows great promise.

Thank you so much for your comments, The Father. I have to admit, this makes me wonder . . .

Yes, child?

I mean . . .

What is it, my child?

This is a weird thing to ask, The Father, I feel uncomfortable even bringing it up.

Tell me, child.

I was just sorta wondering if . . . no, you know what, I can't, forget it, The Father, never mind.

What do you wish to ask of me, child?

It's just—I already know what you'll say, The Father, and you'll be totally right to say it!

Do not presume to know what I will say, Gordon, for I tell ye most forcefully that whatever you may think I am, I am infinitely, yea infinitely, more than that. Simply ask your question, child.

Okay, well, here goes. Your ideas were so right on the money that it made me wonder . . . how would you feel about rewriting these pages, The Father? . . . Hello? . . . Are you still there?

I am pondering your question, my child.

. . . Really?

As you know, I have a tremendous amount to do.

I totally do know that, which is why I didn't think asking you was even a good idea.

Yet ask me you did.

Well yeah, and now I'm embarrassed . . . I'm sorry I brought it up, The Father.

I will do it, my son.

You will??

It sounds like an interesting challenge, and I like those.

That's AMAZING, The Father!

Tomorrow when I come, rather than writing back and forth, as we have done previously, I will, as it were, "puppet" you, my child.

That sounds great, The Father!

Till tomorrow then, child. Get plenty of rest for sometimes when I "puppet" people, I really get "on a roll."

I can't wait, The Father!!

SEVENTH CONVERSATION

The next day The Father came at the planned time and after a few cursory greetings (*How are you today, my child?* Fine, The Father, how are you? *Very well, thank you, are you ready to get going?* Definitely!), The Father began rewriting "Invasion: Earth," through me.

The experience was uncanny, extraordinary. Feeling The Father's power coursing through me, my hands flying across the keyboard, not even being aware of what I was typing, it was profoundly exhilarating. Forty-eight hours after we began, The Father had finished his rewrite, and without any further ado, here it is.

* * *

INVASION: EARTH
By Gordon Whitehead

Chapter One: "It Begins"

It was a Tuesday night. I was in the kitchen, toasting a natural grain english muffin. I'd had a long day at work and I needed some wholesome

sustenance. I turned on the news. Much like any other night here on planet Earth: trouble, strife, unhappiness, and pain. My heart went out to all those suffering and I whispered to myself in empathy and compassion, "Why? Why?"

Then, at the conclusion of the newscast, something unusual. Treated almost as a joke, a story about strange lights in the evening sky, unexplained but probably just the reflection of city lights or a military plane. With a wink and a smile, Mr. Wishing-To-Prove-That-He-Loves-Himself-Yet-Manifestly-Does-Not Newsman let us know it was "nothing serious."

I finished my english muffin with a bit of ghee and drank a glass of full-pulp orange juice, enjoying some of the nourishment which The Father so graciously provides us with, orange juice being just one of the many blessings he offers, blessings so numerous that, were you to attempt to count them, you would need to place the number one with a string of zeroes behind it stretching from Fresno, California to Galveston, Texas and then multiply that number by 400 billion.

Upstairs, Rod Jr lay sprawled on his bed, a book of Native American creation stories across his chest. I smiled knowingly. These stories were only myths, I knew, yet they touched upon something deep and true about the universe. I am Rod Jr's hero, partly because I am a brave firefighter who risks his life on a daily basis, but more so because I used to play professional baseball. I once hit a home run so far that it entered the earth's orbit. After I had the entire left side of my head caved in by a fastball from Clayton Kershaw, however, I was forced to retire. (Little did I know at this point that within two weeks Clayton Kershaw would be gutted like a trout by

under-endowed space aliens.)

Rod Jr's diary was open. My character is far too good to ever look in another person's diary; it is wrong to do so, I tell you, wrong. Yet as Rod Jr wrote in extremely large block letters, I was able to read his diary without it being wrong at all. "Dad is my hero," the page read, "partly because of how he hit that home run into outer space but even more so--and I know this sounds corny, diary, but it's true--because like The Father, Dad is always there for us. Like The Father, Dad would never allow anything bad to happen to us, he would protect us. And I ask ye, diary: Is this not what a father does, protect his beloved children?" I patted Rod Jr on the head and exited.

In our bedroom my wife Maureen, all high full womanly assets and sleepy hair rolled over and looked at me. "What time did Rod Jr go to bed?" "Ten," she said. "Come here." I removed my garments and got into bed next to her. I felt her high, full womanly assets, capped with crinkly peaks the size of men's noses, pressing against my manly chest. Maureen's silky hair whispered against my cheek as she burbled softly, "Give me your mighty manhood, Rod."

I did and Maureen rode a wave of erotic desire towards a waterfall of sensual satisfaction, plunging violently over the waterfall when I pulled out my cellphone and snapped a few photos of her. "Put them on the internet, stud!" she gurgled in my ear. "Fulfill my Inner Truth!" "You bet I will, child," I growled back at her. "You'll be splashed all over the internet." With that, Maureen crashed over the waterfall.

Afterwards as we laid together in holy communion, Maureen started to cry. "What is it, dear child?" I murmured. "I just love you so much,

Rod." "Right back atcha, beloved one." "Let's never let anything change," she babbled. "But dear child, things do change. I tell you it is the very nature of things, for without change we should never grow. Thus should we never fear change, but rather--"

Touching my lips to silence me, Maureen moved her head down towards my re-growing manly asset and began to orally pleasure it. "Yes, dear child," I whispered. "Yessss." Before long we fitted ourselves together like two numbers between five and ten and I do not mean seven or eight, no, I mean six and nine. Maureen and I shared a magnificent session of mutual oral ecstasy; little did I realize at that moment that this would be the last time Maureen and I would 69 for a very long time.

The next day at noon, I was at Subway with my co-worker Oswald, an ambitious young bug-eyed fool. ("Finding Only Outer Love" would surely be his destiny; he would also be gutted like a trout soon.) I was just finishing my side salad with vinaigrette dressing when the skies began to darken. "What's that?" Oswald blabbed, looking up. "Can't say for certain," I replied, "but my intuitive connection with Truth tells me it's not good."

We rushed outside. The beautiful azure sky (yet another of The Father's seemingly endless gifts to mankind; he is so very gracious and kind) was filling with huge, silver spaceships, all of them gliding silently into place, in perfect formation, hovering just above downtown Glendale; a phalanx of gleaming alienness. A strip of bacon hung from Oswald's mouth as he looked up. "What the ...?"

And then a Voice spoke.

(Smiling more broadly than a chessy cat at each of The Father's poetic flourishes, I couldn't wait to see what he'd done with chapter 23.)

Chapter 23: "Brakter Cracks"

"We will destroy you, human, for we need food and your brains, small as they are (and they are small, pathetically so, compared with others in the multiverse), will have to do."

"F you, Braktar," I spat.

"I'm sure you would like to, human, but this shall not occur, I assure you. Rather, very soon your brain will be gurgling in my belly and your body will be nothing but Dust: Denying Un-Scientific Truth."

"There's just one thing you didn't count on, Braktar. No matter how smart and strong you Galtoids may be, we humans never ever give up. Yea, hear me now, Braktar, though we may be frightened, onward we proceed, ever striving to realize IT."

"IT, human?"

"Inner Truth, Braktar. Something that I don't expect an octopus-on-stilts like you could ever understand."

"Hmmn," Braktar prattled, idly stroking his blond goatee. There was a brief moment of clarity in his eyes, then it went away and once again the vile alien was a lost soul. "Bull manure!" he suddenly squawked. "It is all bull manure!"

"First of all, Braktar, bull manure is excellent fertilizer, so when you describe what I said that way, you are actually complimenting my words." Braktar gaped with amazement at my point. "More than that, however, I don't imagine you will find it to be 'bull manure' when that fat green

head of yours splits open like a well-fertilized watermelon hitting hot pavement on a summer day!"

"Listen to me, human," Braktar blathered, leaning close to me, his breath smelling like a mixture of old socks, bad coffee, and dog shit, "you are nothing but a lowly piece of cosmic feces that I have picked up on my space shoe. But space shoes can be cleaned, I say, exactly as brains can be eaten and bodies can turn into Dust: Driving Upon Silent Trails."

In an instant, I knew what was bothering the Alien Leader. "You have a small manly asset, don't you, Braktar?" As he visibly recoiled, I pressed on. "That's it, isn't it? You're under-endowed in the manly asset department and it's poisoned your very soul. You mistakenly believe that the size of the branch determines the value of the tree, yet I tell ye that it does not. It is not because I have an extremely large branch that I am a manly tree, Braktar, no, it is because I act as a hero to others and--"

The pumpkin-headed alien's tentacle suddenly lashed out and slapped me wetly in the face. "Be silent!" he jabbered shrilly. I smiled a cool, tight smile. "I see things clearly now, Braktar. You're not here to eat our brains, you're here to steal our manly assets. Well, listen to me, child: It shall not transpire as ye hope!"

My foot slowly crept towards one of Braktar's lower tentacles. I had to get away from this pencil-penis and save the earth; I was the only one who could (along with my fellow leaders of the Resistance, Generals Bruce Springsteen and Jerry Seinfeld.)

"You amuse me, human. Trapped in a cage you are, with no possible means of escape, yet you continue to threaten me! Hyyaaannhhh hyyyaaannh

hyaaaannnhhh!" Braktar brayed a vile, godless laugh, then pulled out his laser gun and aimed it directly at my head. "Have you any final words, earthman?" he yammered.

"As a matter of fact I do, Braktar: FALL DOWN!!" My foot suddenly shot forward, catching Braktar's leg-tentacle and yanking it out from underneath him. Braktar's profane little mouth formed into a perfect "O" as he clumsily toppled backwards. "Noooooooooo!" he caterwauled as his hateful body hit the floor.

Braktar's keys flew up into the air, exactly as I'd calculated, and right into my hand. Seconds later, I was out of the cage and looking down at Braktar. He gawked up at me, his eyes wide with understanding now. "You possess the power of The Father!" he gurgled desperately. "Please do not use his bottomless powers to harm me!!" "You believed you could steal our manly assets, yet I tell you that what you will actually get is a punch in the face, Braktar!" With that I popped him right in his damned godless face.

Rat-a-tat-tat! Suddenly the Oval Office was swept with bullets as a bunch of Galtoid thugs sporting Uzis burst in and started firing. "Kill him!" yowled Braktar. But I was quick from my years of playing baseball and leapt to the window in a single bound. I could do this because of The Father's love and generosity. Without The Father, I am nothing, nor is anyone else. We are all nothing but for The Father's bottomless love and compassion. Never forget that.

As I jumped out the window I yelled back, "Behold the power of The Father, Fuck-tar!"

***

Fifteen minutes after finishing, I responded to The Father. Our conversation, to put it mildly, did not go as I expected it to.

Wow, The Father.

Yes.

I mean, wow.

Exactly.

It's incredible.

Of course.

Like, breathtaking.

I know.

I love so many of the things you've done.

Tell me, child.

I mean, where to even begin? Braktar is a much better character.

Yes.

So much more textured.

Precisely what I set out to achieve with him, dear one.

I almost sympathized with him at times.

Exactly, child, exactly. What else did you like?

Some of your word choices are just brilliant, The Father.

Be specific, child.

The "waterfall" imagery, for instance, is incredibly poetic.

I know.

And I love the way Bruce Springsteen and Jerry Seinfeld are generals in the Resistance!

Yes.

And so many other things, The Father. I mean, I hope you

won't mind me saying it this way, but your writing is the shit.

Hey now!

I'm sorry. I meant it as a compliment. It's better than bull manure, just to be clear.

I'm kidding, child. I appreciate your praise.

Overall, it's such a tremendous improvement from what it was, The Father! Thank you so much!

You are more than welcome, my child. But tell me: Have you any reservations about the changes I made?

Reservations? Oh my god, no, The Father, not at all!

Certain, are you?

Definitely!

I sense uncertainty in you, my child.

You do?

Indeed.

I mean, there might be a couple of tiny little things I wondered about, The Father.

I sensed this.

But they're nothing really, they're not important at all, just a couple of trivial things that I probably just didn't understand. The headline here is how totally great what you did is, The Father!

Again, I thank you, child, but please understand: I am genuinely interested in your concerns, whatever they might be.

Are you sure, The Father? Because they're seriously not a big deal, they're actually extremely inconsequential.

I wish to hear them, child.

Okay, well, one little thing I'm slightly wondering about,

and I'm not saying this is a bad thing because I don't think it is, at all, but I was kind of struck by how, like, religious the book has become. I mean, I don't have any problem with religion but "Invasion: Earth" was sorta meant to be a fun book, an "airplane book," if you know what I mean, The Father. Now it has this super-religious vibe to it and I'm just not sure—

Gordon.

Yes, The Father?

You are saddening me.

I'm sorry, The Father.

I have begun to transform your novel from a modest little "page-turner" into a document of genuine spiritual significance. Can you possibly be so blind that you do not see this?

No no, I definitely do see it, The Father, it's just that it's, you know, different, that's all.

Of course it is different, child, it is better!

It definitely is, The Father, and I'm super-aware of that, I was just saying . . . I'm really sorry, The Father, I didn't mean to offend you.

I am not "offended," child. As I have told you repeatedly, I am literally not capable of such feelings.

I'm relieved to hear that.

Have you anything else you wish to ask me about my rewrite of "Invasion: Earth"?

. . . Are you sure, The Father?

Proceed, my son.

I'm a little bit curious about a few of your word choices, The Father.

Oh?

Like, there's a lot of "burbling" and "babbling" and "yammering" and "blabbering" and I love that when it's about Braktar, but when it's kind of everybody talking that way . . . I guess I'm just wondering why that is, The Father.

Think ye it's possible that words such as "babbling" and "yammering" convey how your kind sounds to me, child?

Ah. Yes. I see. Right, of course.

Anything else?

I'm maybe not 100% sure about describing Maureen's nipples as "crinkly caps the size of men's noses."

Why not?

Isn't that description kind of . . . bizarre, The Father?

No.

It's not?

Not in the least! It is erotic, Gordon, and correct me if I'm wrong (which as you know is impossible because I am literally never wrong!), but was not "eroticism" what you were striving for in this scene?

It definitely was, but "crinkly caps the size of men's noses" doesn't seem erotic to me; it honestly seems kind of disturbing.

Fine, change it back then! Anything else?

I was wondering why you gave Braktar a blond goatee?

Blond goatees connote villainy, next?

When Rod trips Braktar, you changed, "Have a nice trip, see you next fall" to "Fall down!"

"Have a nice trip, see you next fall" is a hackneyed joke, Gordon. "Fall down!" is simple and commanding.

Really? Because to me it actually seems kind of, I don't know, flat?

You are wrong. It isn't.

It kinda seems like it is to me?

You're wrong, it is sharp and sassy. Next?

After all the euphemisms, it struck me as kind of strange that Rod calls Braktar "Fucktar." It made me wonder, like, what's the point of changing "shit" to "manure" and "penis" to "manly asset" if we're just going to use "Fucktar" in the end anyway?

You know what, Gordon?

What, The Father?

Why don't you just write "Invasion: Earth" exactly the way you damn well please.

That's not what I meant, The Father!

You obviously do not want my help! Do it yourself!

No, The Father!

And while you're at it, I have a new title suggestion for you: "Invasion: Fool!"

Please, The Father, don't say that!

You are not worthy of me wasting any more time on, child!

The Father, no!!

You are most unworthy, in fact, most unworthy!

The Father, please!!

I am leaving now and not coming back!

Don't go, The Father!

But as I depart, I wish to leave you with three final words: Go. To. Hell.

I was wrong, The Father, I love all your changes, I won't change one word, please don't go, I am SOOOO sorry, I won't bring up any of my stupid comments anymore, I never should have said anything, you're vast and wondrous and I'm not even a speck of sand, not even a molecule, I'm NOTHING!! . . . Are you still there, The Father? . . . Hello?? . . . Please??

I sat staring at the computer screen, horrified. Why had I criticized The Father's rewrite of my book? What was wrong with me? Overcome with profound self-recrimination, I couldn't sleep that night, nor the night after, nor the next. In some strange way, after the disastrous ending of this conversation, my life quickly *did* become a kind of hell, exactly as The Father had suggested it would.

Three days later, however, out of nowhere, I was—and there is no other word for it—saved.

EIGHTH CONVERSATION

I am back, child.

The Father??!

Yea, it is I.

Oh my god, The Father, thank you so much for not leaving me forever. I'm so sorry for the idiotic things I said, so ashamed, so—

Hear me now, child.

. . . Yes?

Glad I am that you spoke to me as you did.

. . . Really?

I am not "perfect," dear one. I am capable of "error," just like you. Possible it is, yea, more than possible, that my choice of verbs to describe human speech—"burbling, babbling, blabbering, etc."—though it may convey how your kind sounds to me at times, may also be, let us say, an ungenerous interpretation.

I mean . . .

Also, upon reflection, I see that "Fall down!" is not in fact a good line of dialogue; it is too literal. While I still care not for your line, "Have a nice trip, see you next fall"—

I'm totally not attached to that line, The Father.

—I have in these last few days come to the conclusion that by working together, Gordon, we can and WILL come up with something better.

I'm sorry, are you suggesting that we finish "Invasion: Earth" together, The Father?

That is precisely what I am suggesting, dear one.

You actually want to collaborate with me, The Father??

You are an excellent writer, child.

I am?

Think ye I would collaborate with a "hack"?

Definitely not!

I think you are a gifted storyteller, Gordon, with a sharp ear for dialogue.

Wow! Thanks, The Father!

That you do not possess the depth or wisdom I do is not a criticism of you, child.

Right, because, I mean—who does!?

Who does, precisely? This is how I propose we finish the book, child: You will take the lead and write the final scene of "Invasion: Earth" exactly as you wish; when I have something to contribute, I will briefly step in and "puppet" you, then restore the reins to you as soon as I am done.

I hope you puppet me a lot, The Father!

The amount of puppeting I do will be sufficient, child, no more, no less.

I'm sure it'll be awesome, The Father!

Yes.

Wasting no time, an hour later The Father and I co-wrote

the conclusion to "Invasion: Earth." It was, without a doubt, the most transcendent experience I have ever had. Going back and forth with The Father, writing together in a seamless, effortless manner, our voices blending together so naturally that as I was typing it was honestly difficult for me to see where "I" ended and "The Father" began—it was . . . sublime.

* * *

"Invasion: Earth"
By Gordon Whitehead and The Father

Chapter 32: "MANO A PULPO"

There we stood, Braktar and I, on top of the Washington Monument. As the wind furiously whipped around us, the fat-headed alien sneered viciously, his blond goatee and newly grown Hitler moustache flapping in the breeze. "Did you actually think you could stop me, human?" Braktar sneered. "Ahead of you I have been this entire time and you did not even realize it, hyaaannhh hyaaannhh hyaaannnhh!" On top of everything else, this alien douchebag had a terrible sense of humor. Braktar stopped laughing and looked at me. "Apparently you don't see the humor in this moment, human?" he driveled.

"Oh, don't worry, I'll be laughing real soon, Braktar," I shot back.

"And why's that?"

"Because I'll soon be watching that pumpkin head of yours explode like the watermelon from hell that it is!"

"F you!" Braktar squawked violently, before whipping out a small handheld device. "Know ye

what this is, human?"

"A manly asset extender?"

"F you! No! Within hours, your planet will be completely under our control and your penises will be in a Galtoid 'penis-bank,' from which all brave Galtoid warriors will be able to withdraw and the biggest penis--yours, obviously--will go to ME. But that is not what I hold in my tentacle. Rather, I hold the device that will release millions of warships from the Galtoid mothership, HYAAANNHH HYAAANNNHH HYAAANNH!"

Braktar's tentacle hovered just above a bright red button. If he hit that button, it would represent the demise of humankind. All of our heroic victories in the Great Intergalactic War would instantly be rendered utterly meaningless, these cat-hung space-blasphemers would take over our beautiful planet and wreck it completely. Smirking, Braktar started to do a little victory dance, strutting around and flapping his tentacles, even finishing with a hideous little pirouette. Mock-curtseying, he sneered, "Any final words, human scum?" at me.

"Just this, Braktar. It ain't over till the pumpkin head explodes."

"Wh--?"

I suddenly leapt forward, nimble as a jacked-up baboon, and whipped out the empty beer bottle I'd found moments earlier on top of the Monument and had been hiding behind my back this whole time. Braktar fired his laser gun at me, but I did a backflip in mid-air and landed directly in front of him. He gaped, stunned, "What the f--?" just before I smashed the beer bottle over his fat head. There was a dull thud mixed with a sharp cracking sound and Braktar stood looking at me, wobbly. "It's not possible ..." he gabbled, his

tentacle still poised over that red button.

"You're right, Ass-tar," I growled. "It's not 'possible,' it's 'in-fucking-evitable.'" With that, I jabbed the broken beer bottle at Braktar's face. "Noooooooooo!!" he mewled pitifully as yellow blood spurted out of his saggy chin and cascaded down over his blond goatee. I jabbed at his face again; blood geysered out of his turnip nose and drenched his Hitler moustache. Jabbing a third time, I took off one of his hairy ears. "NOOOOOOOOOOOOOO!!"

Now was the moment of truth. I grabbed Braktar by the collar of his spacesuit and yanked him close. "I told you I was going to watch that godless head of yours explode, Punk-tar, and now I am." Braktar was terrified now, his eyes wide and panicky. "We can work together on this, Rod," he groveled. "I've only been testing you this whole time, I swear."

"Well then, I guess I'm about to flunk, Bitch-tar," I snapped, deftly plucking the device out of Braktar's tentacle as I shoved him backwards off the edge of the Monument. "YAAAAAAHHHHHHHHHHHHH!!!" Braktar shrieked, his tentacles flailing madly as he plummetted. "THIS CANNOT BE, THIS CANNOT BEEEEEEEEEEEEEEEEEEE!!!"

Suddenly, astonishingly, The Father appeared beside Braktar as he fell. The Father was a tall, distinguished gentleman with a thick head of silver hair. He wore a black turtleneck, black slacks, and black cowboy boots. To say that The Father was handsome, well yes, he certainly was, but he was much more than that. He was elegant, he was magnificent, he was, in a word, perfection. Seeing him, Braktar gaped in disbelief. "The Father??"

"Yea, Braktar, I AM The Father."

"Can you help me, The Father??"

"Have ye been Love, Braktar?"

"Uh ... Yes?"

"Ye have not, sinner. Rather, ye have striven for power in a most ignoble way."

Braktar's soul briefly cleared. "Wasted my existence, I have," he whispered.

"Verily ye have, Cuck-tar. Verily ye have." And with that, as quickly as he had appeared, The Father was gone and WHUMP, Braktar hit the ground. Because his head was the heaviest part of his body, it hit the ground first, instantly splattering like an over-ripe honeydew melon.

A bunch of humans instantly attacked Braktar's still-twitching body, yanking its tentacles off and beating his torso with them. General Springsteen strode manfully forward, cut Braktar's beating heart out of his chest, then shot it with a bazooka.

I noticed Rod Jr waving up at me and beaming with pride. "You're the GREATEST, Dad!" I knew he was thinking. Maureen stood next to Rod Jr, one arm around his shoulder, also looking up at me. She licked her lips. "What a MAN Rod is," she was obviously thinking. "I can't wait to give him exactly what he deserves!"

I couldn't wait either, but there was one problem: Earth wasn't saved yet. Hearing a monstrous groaning and creaking sound, I looked up to see the Galtoid mothership, now leaderless and out of control, slowly dropping from the sky. If the ship hit the ground, it would crush everyone there, including Maureen and Rod Jr. I had to act, fast.

As the ship's bow tipped and it started to plummet, my eyes quickly scanned Braktar's device. Because I'd been forced to learn a bit of Galtoid over the past six months I could make out at the bottom of the device two letters: S and D.

"SD," I muttered to myself. What could that stand for? "Semantic Denial"? "Sententious Decline"? "Subliminal Deconstruction"? Then, in a flash, I knew exactly what the letters stood for: "Self Destruct," I whispered to myself. I hit the red button and in a split second, WHOOOOOOSSSHHH, the mothership was gone, vanished forever.

All that remained of the Galtoids was Braktar's tentacle-less body, now being pulled apart by a pack of stray dogs. One of the dogs bit off Braktar's tiny penis and ran away with it. "Not much of a meal, pooch," I quipped as I casually stepped off the side of the Washington Monument and, using my bomber jacket as a parachute, flew down and landed right next to Maureen and Rod Jr.

"Dad!" Rod Jr squealed, hugging me tightly. "How'd you do it, Dad, how'd you defeat Braktar??" "Well, son, the truth is I smashed a freaking beer bottle over his head because sometimes that's the exact right thing to do!" "Awesome, Dad, that's a great lesson, you rule!" We high-fived and then Rod Jr ran off with General Jerry Seinfeld to go defile Braktar's corpse.

"Hey, you." I felt Maureen's hot breath on my neck and half-turned. "Hey back." "That was quite heroic, stud." "Well, you're quite hot, lady." When we kissed deeply, it felt like Maureen's tongue was halfway down my throat, exactly the way I like it. I reached back and grabbed her abundant feminine rear-assets and squeezed them. All was well in the world again, dear ones, all was well in the world again.

Or at least so I thought.

Then I heard something behind me: A hard, cold, metallic voice. "Thank you for doing the hard work for us," the voice droned. I spun around and gasped. There, ten feet away, stood a robot

in a top hat, twirling a cane. "It can't be," I whispered.

"Now it is OUR time to rule, human," the robot jibber-jabbered.

THE END

* * *

Pretty much the moment we finished, The Father and I began to go back and forth excitedly about what we'd just done.

Oh my god, The Father.

Right?

Oh. My. GOD! That last thing with the robot? Unbelievable!

Yes.

I never saw that one coming!

No.

The robot's top hat! What an inspired choice, The Father!

Thank you, child!

It gave the robot such, like, flair.

He is not just any robot, he is the leader of the robots.

And then, oh my god, YOUR appearance!

Yes.

That was mind-blowing.

I know.

Is that actually what you look like, The Father?

Though my essence is, of course, indescribable—

Right, right.

If I did manifest as a human being, yes, that is more or less what I would look like.

I love that you wear cowboy boots and a black turtleneck, The Father!

Comfort AND style, right, dear one?

Exactly! And what a spectacular final moment for Braktar! I love that he finally sees the error of his ways.

But it is too late.

He gets what he deserves!

I enjoyed the dog biting Braktar's penis off, child. I found that most ingenious on your part.

Thanks, The Father!

I also liked Rod's quip.

"Not much of a meal!"

Very clever, child, hahahaha.

Or maybe we should say, "Hyaannhh hyaaannhh hyaaannhh?"

No no, not that, hahaha!

We make a great team, The Father! Did you see that I put your name as a co-writer, by the way?

Yes, and I thank you, child.

It's only fair! You know what was crazy, The Father?

Tell me, child.

There were times when we were writing when I literally had no idea who was making things up. When Braktar started to dance, for instance . . .

A truly marvelous moment.

Right? It was so surprising! You don't think this alien-octopus villain is going to start *dancing* near the climax of the book and then when he does—

It is pure magic.

It really is!

Braktar's dance was us working in perfect harmony, my child.

I have to admit that while we were writing, I couldn't stop thinking about this as a movie, The Father.

I completely understand.

For Rod, I was instantly going to Costner.

Costner would be perfect.

And what do you think about Halle Berry for Maureen, The Father?

A marvelous idea, child! As for Braktar, there is one and only one choice: Sean Penn.

Oh man, I love Sean Penn!

He would be utterly magnificent.

But who would play you, The Father?

Al Pacino, dear one.

That's interesting, I sort of imagined someone taller like, I don't know, Harrison Ford maybe?

How many Oscars does Harrison Ford have, my child?

Oh, yeah, that's true.

Also, I was not done: Imagine Al Pacino in platform cowboy boots.

Fantastic! One thing we know for sure is who'll do the music, right?!

Bruuuuuuuuuuuuuuuce!!

Indeed!

"Indeed," hahaha, a very good one, child.

Thank ye, The Father!

Yet another good one! And now, beloved one, as I suggested earlier, it is time for you to Graduate.

What does that mean, The Father?

It is time for you to convey our marvelous communication to the world, Gordon!

I want to, The Father!

It is imperative that mankind hear what we have to say and quickly, child.

I totally get that, The Father!

You DO get it, child, and there is a reason for that: Because you have found IT.

. . . Inner Truth? . . . I have?

Verily, my child.

I'm . . . wow . . . no words, The Father . . .

No words are necessary, dear one.

I'm just . . . so happy, The Father.

This will make you even happier, child: Now that you have finally found IT, we can, together, begin to find OUT!

. . . Out, The Father?

"Our Unique Truth."

Seriously??

Seriously indeed, Gordon Whitehead!

When can we start to find OUT, The Father? I want to keep going right now?!

When the time is right, my son, you will know it. Until then, go ye forth into the world and spread the word, child!!

I will, The Father! And thanks! I love you!

Right back atcha, dear one. Ciao!

EPILOGUE

And that was it.

Six months have passed. I actually did get in some fairly serious legal trouble for the beer bottle thing. I had to get a job at Walmart and move home with my parents for awhile to pay the legal fees. My parents are talking about charging me rent. If I didn't know they were "empty boats" who will quite soon "pass," it would probably bother me. I haven't talked to Brent in five months; the last thing he said to me was "I hate you and I always will." I'm giving him some space. Joan hasn't forgiven me for posting the sex photos of her on the internet. She's threatening to sue me too. I'm pretty sure she's bluffing. I'm trying to sell "Invasion: Earth," but I haven't had any luck yet. (Though I have moved on to the sequel, "Invasion: Earth Two—Robocalypse.") Overall, I'd have to say that the humility The Father prescribed for me has come in plenitude. And yet, somehow, out of all this humility has come a hard-earned understanding of Inner Truth.

And so, dear friends, as we part, I wish you the same thing: Utter humiliation that leads to IT.

Be Love.

ABOUT THE AUTHOR

Gordon Whitehead is a contemporary spiritual explorer. He is currently working on the follow-up to "Conversations with The Father," "Arguing with The Father (and Winning!)" He is also currently developing "Invasion: Earth: The Rise of FL-241-X" as a web series. Gordon lives in Simi Valley, California, with his two cats, Neil Donald Walsch and Maurice.

ABOUT THE AUTHOR

Chris Matheson is a screenwriter whose credits include the *Bill & Ted* movies and *Rapture-Palooza*. He is also the author of *The Story of God*, *The Trouble with God*, and *The Buddha's Story*. He lives in Portland, Oregon.